Dedicated to Lois Annet
The following is a poem written

Tree in the Lake

The mountains and the valleys expected
The trees on top of the hill,
But the tree in the middle of the lake
I seen makes me shake my head.
The tree in the middle of the late,
I see
The tree I see, I think
It could be an illusion. the tree
in the middle of the lake
The waves have battered and broken it.
The wind sweeps over the lake
Shaking and shivering it stands and lives,
The tree in the middle of the lake.
It reminds me of one indestructible
Its branches a home for the birds.
It holds its course no matter how hard.
The winds and waves roll by,
Its arms reach up to the sun above.
Is it seeking an answer from the deep, dark space?
The tree in the middle of the lake
A symbol of time and space.

This poem written by my mom is symbolic of both our lives. How interesting!.. My mom, one of eight children, raised in a hotel, where every day at lunch she had to run back to the hotel to serve the

clients lunch and then get back to school. She was one of the Annett girls in a small town on the Gaspe coast of Quebec, Canada.

Lois Annett Gilker was a teacher of unconditional love. Thank you mom for that. She married my father when she was 20 years old and by 30 had 6 children. I was the last one. Such an amazing woman raising 6 children, running a restaurant and store, and dealing with challenging husband. She was a smart/savvy business woman, who never really got to develop her talents except with a small babysitting agency she started and later sold. She was a substitute teacher and ended working full time because of the demands for her abilities doing this. My mother always did whatever it took to make a healthy, happy life for her children.

The things I remember most about my mom is how she loved my daughter Bree. Whenever, I visited my parents, as soon as I walked through the door – her arms were out and the first words out of her mouth were –Give me my girl………….. Bree would spend long periods of time sitting, snuggled with my mom in the rocking chair.

My mother, I know was very scared for me and the journey I had ahead with Bree, yet she did a pretty good job of hiding it. Every parent wants their children's lives to be easier and she knew that I had a tough road ahead.

Thank you Mom, I hope I made you proud.

The decisions that you make
And the actions that you make
Upon the Earth are the means by which you evolve.
At each moment you choose the
Intentions that will shape your
Experience and those things upon which
You will focus your attention.
These choices affect your Evolutionary
Process. This is so for each person.
If you choose unconsciously, you evolve
unconsciously.
If you choose consciously, you evolve
consciously.

– "The Seat Of The Soul"
by Gary Zukav

Table of Contents

Preface

When I was given a brain-injured daughter, I desperately sought answers to the difficult situation. My story is written for the parents of brain-injured children, parents who are given an opportunity to participate in a wonderful learning experience, a chance to make a meaningful life for their children. I hope to show them that along a road less traveled lies powerful healing.

The reader will meet a wonderful little girl who has taught her mother some of life's most important principles: the meaning of life, why we are here, and the importance of being truly human. She has been her mother's most important and greatest teacher. Her very existence forced her mother to make an exhaustive research study of the conditions affecting children with her problem.

This book is also for anyone who comes in contact with one of these children. Each child is precious and should be cherished. No one should fear or have any negative response to a brain-injured child. My earnest hope is that reading my story will not only change any preconditioned reactions, but also show that unconditional love can work wonders.

Swan

Chapter 1

> For a moment I hated a six-year-old boy whose name I didn't even know.
> All he had done was what thousands of children had before him. He had
> yelled a thoughtless taunt to his friend, but the words seared my very
> soul. "Stop acting like a retard!" That was what he shouted to his friend.

Walter and I were married in the summer of 1977. We were born and grew up in Canada and our first home was a beautiful Swiss-chalet style house overlooking a lake, just five miles from the ski resort of St. Sauveur Des Monts where Walter was the director of the ski school. He was an excellent downhill skier, good enough to have been a member of the Canadian National B Ski Team. I was a certified downhill instructor. We were both quite health-conscious, keeping fit by running and cross-country skiing.

Life was treating us very well. We were living a "golden life"; a carefree, wonderful lifestyle that allowed us to travel, to meet people with similar interests and tastes and to live pleasantly with few restrictions. There were fun times with trips to Europe: downhill skiing in France, working Ipso (a sporting goods show) in Germany, and cross-country skiing in Finland. We had been together for four years and I was twenty-eight. The time seemed right for starting a family, yet I had one question about making this decision. It was a faint echo of my feelings in the seventies when I had wondered whether it was right to bring a child into a world that seemed to be falling apart, with no one doing anything about it. I had read Eric Fromm, Alan Watts, Herman Hesse, Fritz Perls, and Aldous Huxley, but at that time I was too young to fully understand their concepts.

As I got older, the questions of my youth faded. *Anyhow*, I thought, *What can one person do to change anything as immense as the problems of the world?* I decided to suggest to Walter that we have a child. He was not enthusiastic about my suggestion but willing to go along with my proposal. I had my IUD removed. An unplanned pregnancy in the past had resulted in a miscarriage. When I became pregnant again, all progressed smoothly.

I wasn't worried about the coming child, health-wise. Our family history was good, with my mother being one of eight healthy children and my father one of six. Walter's family also had a history of healthy births – and long lives; One of his grandmothers had recently died at the age of ninety-seven. My immediate family was in good health. I am the youngest of six children, all of whom had been born at home without and complications.

I wanted a girl and had already made up my mind that the baby I was carrying was of that sex. I had selected her name even before she was conceived… one that was beautiful and could not be shortened into a nickname: Bree. Walter was an interested onlooker as I dived into the anticipation of motherhood. Friends were amused by my unconscious habit of rubbing my very pregnant belly, as if I was telling Bree that she was safe and that I loved her. I knitted sweaters, borrowed a beautiful little family wooden crib, and read all the relevant books I could find. This would be a first grandchild on Walter's side of the family but the sixth on mine, so there were plenty of baby items passed on to us.

Walter learned about the frustrations of a woman who is eight months pregnant and feeling abandoned. His was a fun job which involved lots of skiing. I worked at the making office during the weekend but didn't want to hang around the bar. I wanted to be home nesting. One evening he called to say that he'd be home late for supper. He planned to have a couple of beers with some of the instructors… again. Walter arrived home half an hour later than he said he would. Our dog, Sam, had a supper of pork chops, homemade mushroom sauce, a baked potato, and fresh veggies. Sam thought he had died and gone to heaven!

I had been seeing a doctor in Montreal, but with all proceeding normally, he recommended I switch to a doctor closer to home. So for the last month I saw one in Ste. Agathe, just eight miles away. I made arrangements to go to the small Ste. Agathe hospital instead of the much larger one in Montreal. This seemed advantageous in more ways than one. It would be easier for Walter to visit and, in a smaller hospital, attention was likely to be more personal. Later, I would regret this decision I had made because of Walter's insistence.

Walter had been taking natural childbirth classes with me and we felt well prepared for March 17th, 1980… which came and went with no arrival. I had heard all sorts of stories about late arriving babies and carried some of these tales to my doctor. He reassured me that he wasn't worried, but he did suggest an X-ray to check things out. All the X-ray confirmed was that he head was not yet engaged, nothing unusual. I mentioned that I didn't think the baby moved much, but I had nothing to compare this with and the moment passed. My only discomfort was caused by painful hemorrhoids. I was told this was not unusual during pregnancy.

April first: Walter's grandmother's birthday. I was making frequent trips to the bathroom. Walter went to bed early, at about eight, and shortly after I made another trip to the bathroom. This time it was different. The bowl seemed full of blood. My mind raced. Was this the show I had heard about? Was the baby finally on the way? Should I go to the hospital? I needed feedback so I woke Walter. He suggested calling the nurse from our birthing class. She advised us to go to the hospital – just to be sure.

There was the usual procedure at the hospital. After a general checkup, the doctor recommended I stay overnight and that if nothing happened during the night I would be induced the following afternoon. I asked Walter to stay with me because I didn't want to be left alone. It was our first and I didn't know anyone… and no one seemed to know what was really happening. He was not enthusiastic but did so because of my fears. He dozed on another bed in the pre-delivery room.

The next day induction was started. When a nurse tried to insert a needle for an IV in my arm, she had problems. After six unsuccessful attempts, a doctor came and did it. This incident concerned me. Here I was about to have my first child and nothing was proceeding normally. The nurse couldn't do a simple thing like getting a needle into my arm. Did these people know what they were doing?

Four hours after induction was started, there was no progress. The baby's head was not engaged. The doctor consulted my former doctor in Montreal by phone and it was decided that if there was still no progress by the following morning, I would be transferred to the larger hospital in Montreal. Walter went home to get a good night's sleep. It was arranged that he would go directly to Montreal's St. Justine Hospital the next day.

This was not the way I had envisioned having this baby. For twenty-four hours professionals were working in me, around me, on me. Nobody was working with me. I had many questions but received no answers. I was naïve. I had no idea how our lives were about to change, how everything we had planned for the future would be so drastically altered.

April fool's day! Was this some weird joke on me?

Chapter 2

Thank God for Gillian, a nurse at Ste. Agathe, because without her watchful care, Bree would not be with me today. She was concerned because every time I went to the bathroom, bleeding would start. She took it on herself to call the doctor at home and alert him about my problem. He arrived with a surgeon and I learned that they had been talking to my Montreal doctor, The decision was made to perform a Caesarian. They gave me a choice: either to have the operations right away, in which they could guarantee both my life and the life of my baby, or I could wait until morning and go as arranged to Montreal. If I chose the latter, they could not guarantee the life of my baby. There was, of course, no choice to be made. I wanted Walter to come to the hospital immediately. I didn't want to face the operation alone.

A Caesarian! God, how could this be happening? I was one of the healthiest members of our class and had never been sick, had never even liked visiting people in hospitals. The prospect of having an operation was frightening. I was scared, really scared! When I was stripped, shaved, and lying nude on the operating table with my stomach painted a mud color, I felt like a piece of meat. Strangers were working on me – like mechanics on a car. My whole body was shaking and I was cold. They injected a drug and my fear intensified. Was body was chilling. *I'm dying,* I thought, *and I can do nothing about it!* The next thing I remember was sitting bolt upright and saying,

"Oh God, it hurts!" Another shot. The next thing I remember is seeing Walter walking beside me as I was being taken to my room. My impression was fuzzy. There was something wrong… very wrong.

Walter's Words:

I got the call and immediately dressed and started my frantic drive back to the hospital. It took me nearly twenty-five minutes to get there and by the time I arrived I was over my panic, After all, friends had gone through having Caesarians and their children were perfectly healthy.

I parked in the hospital lot just before midnight. It was quiet and peaceful. I saw no one as I went up to the maternity ward. A nurse told me that Wendy had already been taken to the operating theater. I had always planned to be in the labor room during the birth, so it seemed natural to the operating theater to be with her there. I was wrong. Hospital policy kept me outside and I sat alone in a small alcove but not for long. The pediatrician came out and I saw he was extremely shaken and nervous, He fumbled for a cigarette and his voice quavered.

"Something is wrong. Something is wrong with the baby." I remained calm because his words were not registering. "We had to work for twenty minutes to get her to breath. Something is not right with your daughter." I felt it hard to relate to the baby. It was Wendy I was worried about.

"What about my wife?"

"She's fine. She's still under anesthesia, but she's fine."

Now the shock of the doctor's first words came through to me. I had left the hospital earlier full of anticipation about the impending birth of our child. I trusted the doctor's competence and that of the hospital staff. All appeared to be under control and, with no previous experience in these matters, I had no suspicion that it might not be. Now, my wife was alive and appeared to be in no danger, but our newborn baby had taken twenty minutes to breath and had something wrong with her! I was not getting the information I needed. The doctor seemed to be a mess. Perhaps he felt guilty about the traumatic birth or perhaps he had never seen complications of this sort before. Whatever the reason, it was causing me great confusion.

Together, we looked through a glass window into the Intensive Care Ward where the baby was in an incubator. He told me that she was very small and that something was wrong with her left eye.

"She has some kind of strange look," was the way he put it. "But she is stable and breathing on her own."

I took what comfort I could from that. The words "something is wrong" had not yet sunk in. I was thinking purely of some sort of physical problem – and, after all, there are operations and therapy for a multitude of physical problems. It was well past midnight and the doctor was telling me there was nothing we could do other than wait and see how she did. He said Wendy was back in her room and my attention was switched entirely to her and what I could tell her. What could I tell her? I didn't know what the hell was wrong with our daughter. I began walking down the long corridor that led to her room and I met her being wheeled back to her room.

Wendy:

I was back in what seemed to by my room and Walter was there. He looked as if he had been crying. I asked him if everything was alright. He said that he was happy because the baby was the little girl I had wanted so badly. I guessed that everything was fine and that it was just the drugs that were making me feel so strange... and then I passed out again. That night was a long one of waking up to nurses checking on me, giving me shots, and short periods of sleep. After two days with very little sleep and lots of stress, I was exhausted.

Morning came and I was ready to see Bree. The nurses were oddly uncommunicative and would not bring her to me. The doctor was nowhere to be found. I felt I was getting the run around. All the information I could get from the nurses was that Bree was rather small and there seemed to be a problem with one of her eyes. Nothing to worry about. I had been seeing an eye doctor since I was three. One of my brothers had been born with both eyes crossed and an operation had soon corrected the problem. What was the big deal? I wanted to see my daughter, wanted to hold her.

Walter came to tell me there was some problem with our baby and the doctors wanted to transfer her to St. Justine's for more specialized care. They were stressing her small size and low weight. I would be allowed to see her for ten minutes before they sent her to Montreal.

Things were moving so fast and I wasn't allowed to be part of the decision making, All I wanted was to be able to hold my little girl and keep her safe, but she was being swept away and no one would give me a reason. The incubator was wheeled into my room. She was so tiny... asleep and so sweet. I touched her head and then wondered why her ears were so flat against it. Where they stuck? No matter, that could be fixed. She was so beautiful, my little girl. Everything would be alright, somehow, now that I had seen her.

They came to take her away. God, It wasn't ten minutes! I was afraid that somehow they might actually lose her, my little daughter all alone. They assured me that a nurse would be with her all the way to the Montreal Hospital. I was planning to breastfeed her and I insisted that she would be fed with my milk, that Walter would take it to Montreal. I learned later that the nurses thought it was a little strange. Here I was with a brain-damaged child and all I was worried about was breast-feeding. They didn't realize how little I knew at that moment, that I was unaware of her serious condition.

The next few days were a blur. My world was falling apart and I had no idea what to do about it. No one was talking to me, no one was giving me a straight answer. Indeed, they were acting as if I was stupid... and they were doing it in French. Now, French is my second language and I am quite fluent in it, but, when your life is upside down, you want to hear your mother tongue.

It is still hard for me to recall much of the first few days after Bree's birth. It was a time of confusion, of bits and pieces, and of being given pain shots. One evening a nurse came in to persuade me to talk or cry it all out. I didn't know what "it all" was. It wasn't as if my baby had died. My parents called and I had little to tell them except that Bree was in Montreal and I could do nothing until I got out of the hospital. My Mom said she would come. My sister called and said she loved me and I cried.

Dean, and old friend, called with congratulations. Yes, I had my little girl, but something was wrong with her. I didn't know what the problem was. My cousin Valerie and her parents drove a long way to see me. Friends who lived closer stayed away when they heard something was wrong.

The only clear memory of those early days is how I felt when I finally saw Bree. I loved her from the first moment, and overwhelming surge that took my by surprise. God, I would kill to protect this child. I had never felt that kind of love before. She looked so tiny, so defenseless. It was easy to love her. She was my beautiful baby. I felt like a mother tiger. About fifteen years later I found out from reading a book on Chinese horoscopes that my sign was a tiger. The key characteristics of this sign are that the tiger has humanitarian instincts; when involved, the involvement is total. The tiger is never halfhearted about in endeavor and always gives one hundred percent of herself and even more when she can. These characteristics were a foundation of what I would need to cope with what was ahead of me. God knew I had to be born in the year of the tiger.

Another day or two and I was in discomfort, then real pain with my swollen breasts. The nurses had not taken seriously my intention to breastfeed. Or perhaps they thought Bree might not live.

A pediatrician appeared in my doorway. He seemed reluctant to enter. He wore a huge wooden cross around his neck and, at first, I thought he was a priest. I asked him what was wrong with my daughter and met evasion: Perhaps it was just a small eye problem, perhaps it could be serious enough to mean institutionalization. They just didn't know yet.

INSTITUTIONALIZATION! That was the word I heard, a word that was not part of having a baby, Our child institutionalized? Was this some kind of weird joke? What was God thinking of? This was something that happened to other people… not a normal, healthy couple like us. I didn't smoke or drink or eat junk food. My pregnancy had been normal, better than most. Why was God punishing me? I couldn't understand this. I equated institution with a prison and one does not put a little baby in prison. How could this doctor be using that word in relation to my little daughter?

My own doctor finally got up the nerve to see me three days after Bree was born. He admitted outright that he had been afraid to face me. I remember his visit very well. He sat across from me, a total wreck. All he was able to tell me was that Bree had been sent to Montreal so she could have better care. She was only four pounds, six ounces and could not go home until she weighed five pounds. He had nothing to offer me. It seemed as if he only came so I could make him feel better, rather than the other way around. He kept telling me how good Walter had been . Walter must have made a good impression on him the night Bree was born… probably because he did not blow up at the doctor that night.

Walter was my link to Bree. He took my milk to her and told me the nurses were being attentive to her, that she was getting good care. I felt that my milk was very important, that she especially needed it because of her low birth weight. I hoped it would give her the best chance to deal with whatever lay ahead. Also, I needed to feel that I was helping Bree. It was what was keeping me together especially emotionally. Being in the hospital without Bree was extremely depressing. Other women came in and had their babies and I heard them calling relatives with the wonderful news. I felt like a freak; In the maternity ward with no baby to show for it. I persuaded the doctors to let me go home early. My only regret is that I didn't go to Montreal with Bree. This was not presented as an option and things were happening so fast that in my confusion, this possibility didn't occur to me. I would have needed someone else to make decision for me.

Bree and I were separated for our first eight days and during that stretch Walter was dealing with family and friends, trying to give answers he didn't have. At the ski resort where he worked, he was constantly being asked about the situation… and then there was the time he spent travelling between the two hospitals. What a way to start a family! It was a great relief to him when the doctors agreed to discharge me. He took a couple of days off.

Driving home without a baby was not the way we had imagined the return trip. Were the last five days real or was it a nightmare? How could one's life change so drastically in just five days? It was between seasons when the snow was not quite gone and everything looks muddy. I felt empty and drained. Spring is a time of rebirth and here we were between seasons with no clear idea of what was in store for us. I don't remember if we talked much on the drive home. There was so little either of us could say.

Why couldn't I wake from this nightmare?

Arriving home without Bree felt strange. Our dog, Sam, was overjoyed to see us, but his excitement did little to cheer me. Only having my daughter with me could have moved me. Bree's crib was made up and reader for her, right next to our bed. Her clothes were neatly folded on the bureau and there was a supply of diapers reader to be used. I was still pumping milk and Walter was taking it to Montreal. He had brought me pictures so that I could at least visualize her.

My parents arrived the day after I came home from the hospital. My Mom had made plans to stay with me a couple of weeks to help me adjust to the new routine. She was confused because of the situation and tried to put the blame somewhere. My father kept saying that Bree would grow out of "it."

The time that elapsed between my homecoming and Bree's is still a blur. There were still so many questions going through my mind with no answers given. We were not being told what to expect of Bree. This was a strange new world for us and we had no idea how we were supposed to act. It was a time of total confusion. I had given birth to a wonderful new little human being, and yet there was one thing I dreaded... a MENTALLY RETARDED CHILD. I had been told that we had a child who would never grow up, would always need to be cared for. What if the doctor was right and Bree needed to be put in an institution? How could we let our little baby, a part of each of us, be put away away from us in a place she would never leave? I had been so careful to follow all the doctor's instructions. Why had this happened? Was it some kind of punishment?

I wanted my baby to come home as soon as possible so I could nurse her and keep her safe. My overwhelming fear was that she might die in the hospital. I desperately wanted her to life. It didn't matter that she was not perfect. She was my little girl. No one gives you and guarantees when you decide to have a baby, yet the gift is a living, breathing part of you, desperately needing love. My maternal instinct was strong and I felt that somehow things would work out. The first step was to get her home.

I had to know how Walter felt.

"What if the doctors and right and we have to put her in an institution?" His response was a relief.

"If it comes to that, Bree won't even know who we are. But for now, we should bring her home and see what happens."

A call from the hospital informed us that the magic weight of five pounds had been achieved and we could bring Bree home. I packed clothes and blankets. The trip to Montreal seemed to take much longer than usual. I worried that I would not recognize Bree. Water thought I was being silly, yet he had been seeing her every day and so he knew her better than I did. He didn't seem to comprehend that the mother-daughter bonding had not taken place. The whole birthing process had been far from normal and I felt shy and insecure about meeting my daughter even though it was what I wanted more than anything in the world. The only time I had seen her was under traumatic circumstances and it felt strange not to know my own daughter. I felt lost.

Walter was very much at home in the hospital and he took me to the second floor where Bree shared a room with five other babies. I searched each face hoping to recognize her from Walter's photos. Once I saw her knew she was out little girl, so tiny and sweet. She was asleep and looked just like any other little baby.

There were papers to be signed and a doctor to see, so we left her clothes with a nurse. The doctor took blood samples and asked questions about our family histories. He was unable to give us any answers but said they would search for genetic causes. Until they received the results of the tests that were to be made, there was little that could be added to the small amount of informations we had been given.

The nurse had already started dressing Bree by the time we returned and I quickly took over. The clothes were the smallest I could find and yet they were huge on Bree. I talked continuously while I dressed her. Only then did I realize how much I had missed being with her and how much a part of me she was. I was still weak and Walter went to hunt up a wheelchair to take me downstairs. It felt wonderful to leave with Bree in my arms.

This was the beginning of our being parents. The hospital had no place in this picture. It seemed very important to get Bree away from its atmosphere as soon as possible, so we could strive for a normal life. Once she was in my arms, I felt more secure, more in control.

My parents were eagerly awaiting our arrival. Mom took one look at Bree and saw only her newest grandchild all ready to be loved and held. She would be the only member of my family to love Bree unconditionally over the years that followed. Bree was loved just because she was here, one more grandchild to be cherished. Whenever they were together, my mother would hug her, rock her and kiss her, telling her how how much prettier she had grown. They spent hours in the rocking chair with Mom taking Bree's face in her hands and telling her how sweet it was. Bree was always content when she was with my Mom.

But that was all in the future. In the meantime, we were newly home. Pictures we took of the homecoming were so heart-rending – Walter and I so traumatized and Bree looking as though she had survived a battle – that I later destroyed them.

I didn't see my doctor again until six weeks later. I took Bree for a routine checkup. In answer to my persistent questions, I was able to get more information from him although he seemed reluctant to tell me anything. At birth the amniotic fluid had turned green, the placenta was calcified, and the umbilical cord had been wrapped around her body three times. The doctor said that if she had remained in my body another hour or two, she would not have lived at all. One question he seemed to think was important was whether Bree was having regular bowel movements. When I said she was, he guessed that everything inside her was working properly. Other than that, he didn't seem to have much interest in her. I was being the Proud Parent and he acted as though the sooner we were gone, the better. I guess we had made a dent in his perfect birth record.

Mom had stayed with us six weeks, knowing she was needed and Dad busied himself with odd jobs, returning home from time to time to attend to things there. It was Mom I needed most for support at the time. Bree had to be fed every two hours and she adjusted very well to breastfeeding in spite of our eight-day separation. I focussed on getting my strength back. I planned to continue breastfeeding for a year and I knew I would have to be feeling fit to do that.

Walter was thinking about practical things and he decided we needed a new car. The one he bought was a four-wheel drive Subaru which would be excellent because we lived five miles from the small ski village of St. Sauveur des Monts on a dead end gravel road. I am sure he was thinking of a car that would get his family through a Canadian winter, but for me it was just another problem, U had standard shift and I found myself having to learn to drive all over again. I was impatient about having to practice. It was complicated enough having to deal with a new baby with an unknown future and possible problems and now I had to learn to drive a car with a standard shift. One more stressful situation I did not need. Didn't I have enough to do? I guess I took a lot of my inner anger out on that car. Looking back to that time, it was probably good to have had that opportunity to vent my emotions.

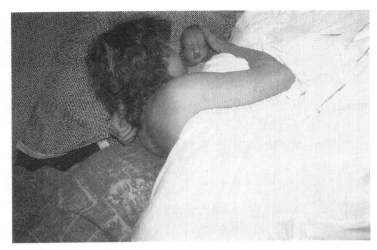

First night home (above)

Bree and her father, first five days (above)

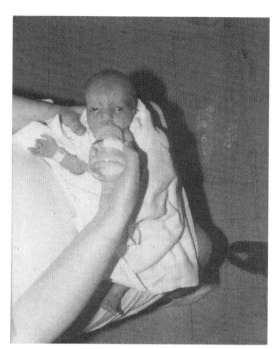

Bree at hospital being fed my
milk by the nurse,
First five days (left)

First day home in
Rocker with me (right)

Arriving home first day (left)

Bree with my mother, Lois (below)

Bree with her Grandmother and Grandfather Scofield (left)

Chapter 3

Bree was born on April 2nd and that first couple of months were spent trying to establish a routine, maintaining the house keeping myself together, and snatching sleep whenever I could. It was not until June 8th that she slept as long as six hours for the first time. I was feeling like a zombie. An incident that happened one night illustrates my mental state, an indication of the stress I was feeling. Bree had awakened at 2 a.m. and I took her into the living room to feed her so I wouldn't disturb Walter. I went back to bed. A little later I awoke in a cold sweat, positive that I had left Bree in the living room alone. Of course I hadn't. she was tucked into her crib by my side of the bed, safe and sound. Relief surged through me as I saw her there.

There was a period in July when Bree seemed to scream non-stop for four straight days. Mom gave me some practical advice. She thought Bree was probably hungry and suggesting adding some solid food, like creamy cereal, to her diet. This proved to be my answer. It seemed strange that so small a baby could need such large quantities of food. Then I was told that her assimilation was poor and food went in and out at a rapid state. She was not getting the necessary nutritional benefits from the food and consequently required larger amounts to survive.

When Bree was two months old, we finally learned the cause of her problems. A genetics specialist at St. Justine's said it was Wolf-Hirschhorn Syndrome, also known as 4p- Syndrome. This meant that a small piece is missing on that short arm of her fourth chromosome. He showed us a medical book with a write-up on this particular condition which had only been identified in the mid-seventies. The article spoke about a short life span, a cry that sounded like a cat's, and a helmet-shaped head. There were only twenty-five known cases in North

America. I got a photocopy of the article but no matter how often I read it, I had difficulty relating it to Bree.

I asked the doctor why it had taken so long to diagnose Bree and he was at a loss. He said he could have identified the problem within five minutes of seeing her, a statement that showed an enormous lack of communication within the hospital, in my estimation. The tests done on Walter and me proved negative, so it was not a question of heredity. The doctor added that there was a one in a million chance of this happening. Then he told us to make an appointment to see an eye specialist because Bree's left eye had an off-center pupil. This was the first and only doctor who gave us definite and factual information.

Two weeks later I was told by the eye specialist that she could not make a full examination of the eye unless Bree was put to sleep. That really troubled me. It had taken so long for Bree to start breathing on her own at birth that I was not keen on the idea of subjecting her to an anaesthetic unless it was absolutely necessary. The doctor said that it was. Bree could become blind in that eye if nothing was done to correct the problem. I said I would think about it.

Back at home, I contacted Dr. Ramsey, the doctor who had been treating my family's eye problems for years. His secretary gave me a hard time, indication that the doctor was too busy to fit us in. I did something I would never do under normal circumstances: I called him at home. When he heard my story, he didn't sound happy with his secretary. He referred me to Dr. Little, a specialist at Montreal Children's Hospital. He took two hours to examine Bree without anesthesia. Over the next few years, we had many visits there. Every couple of months there was a doctor to see, an examination to be made. These were all routine procedures. Although we were quite inexperienced, we soon learned what questions to ask and what procedures to dispute. The orthopedic department learned that we did not want Bree to be given X-rays automatically before she was even examined. The therapists were a little taken aback the first time we questioned the necessity; after all, it was routine. We insisted on being given a better reason that that. Surprisingly, they were able to examine Bree at least ninety-nine percent of the time without the need for X-rays.

Bree's first year of life involved one medical appointment after another. Walter and I had many emotional adjustments to make. There were the negative reactions of friends and family members and ever present trauma about having a child who was not supposed to live long and who would not lead a normal life for the short period she would be with us. I searched for anything I could do to help my baby.

We tried to live as full a family life as we could. We took Bree everywhere with us. When she was two months old, we visited our friends Barb and Jack Nash in Stowe, Vermont. They, bless them, acted normally with Bree and have continued to do so over the years. There has never been any strain during our visits at their home.

When Bree was five months old, we decided to take a vacation for a week at a cabin we had on Gaspe Peninsula in the Province of Quebec. My family is from a small town called New Carlisle and many of my relatives still lived there. We wanted the vacation before the start of the ski season when Walter would be busy. It rained most of the week, yet it felt good to get away from St. Sauveur and pretend we were just a regular couple on vacation with their baby.

I packed the nutritional reference books which were my guides – *Feeding Your Child* by Louise Lambert-Lagace and *The Complete Guide to Preparing Baby Foods At Home* by Sue Castle. I had just started Bree on vegetables and I was also giving her vitamin supplements (C and B6) and Brewer's yeasts. Her course of vaccinations had also been started.

I had been earning a little extra money on the side sewing ski hats and the four hundred dollars a month I made from that paid for our new mortgage. I had an old industrial sewing machine and Bree grew accustomed to its sound (She loves the sound of the vacuum cleaner today and I feel it's because this is the closest noise she hears that is like that of the old sewing machine). I was yet to read books on the effects of different sounds on healing and later *The Secret Life of the Unborn Child* by Thomas Verdy which describes how the baby in the womb is very much aware of the sounds from three-months gestation on. If I had known about that during my pregnancy, I would have been listening to classical music and reading inspirational books aloud instead of working on an industrial sewing machine.

It was during November that I noticed something that frightened me very much. Bree seemed to have brief lapses, lasting one to five seconds. At first I thought it might be my imagination. I watched her like a hawk. By December I knew it was not a figment of my imagination and I was sure she was having seizures, even though I had never seen one. There is a myth about mothers that says they don't admit to what they don't want to see. This is totally incorrect. It is usually the mother who tells the doctor something is wrong with her child when the doctor continues to state that everything is fine. Most mothers are honest about what is happening to their children. I insisted something was decidedly wrong.

An E. K. G. at the Children's Hospital proved I was right. Bree was having seizures. It was decided to hold back on drugs to see what might develop. The doctor said that Bree was severely brain-damaged and had little chance of living beyond the age of five. An appointment was made with the head of the neurology department. This doctor, a woman, was a disappointment to me. I had hoped for a womanly compassion and understanding, but she was cold and reserved. She said Bree would not be able to move, would be a vegetable, and would be lucky to live to the age of five. Nonetheless, she did not need to be hospitalized...yet!

I was devastated. I went home and cried for three days. After crying myself out, I resolved to prove that woman wrong. She had used the word "hospitalized", but what she had meant was permanent institutional care. Well, there was no way anyone was going to put my child away! My meeting with that doctor fueled my burning desire for information and answers and all my spare time was spent looking for alternatives.

During my search I discovered a library in Montreal at the Mentally Retarded Association and I borrowed all their books that seemed to indicate there were possibilities other than institutionalization. Many books were written about Down's Syndrome children and outlined stimulation methods. I read through them all.

In the meantime Walter was trying to make his own adjustments.

Walter:

Friends with children had told me they grow up before you know it. One minute they're in diapers and the next they're off to kindergarten. Well, this was not the case with Bree. At one year she weighed only thirteen pounds and a pillow was large enough for her mattress. She made a few sounds, could not speak, and had no mobility. I began to realize how far behind she was falling. Each day, watching helplessly while Bree lay there unable to do the simplest things that babies do was the hardest thing of all. I'd think, *If only she would move about, show some interest in her surroundings... do SOMETHING!*

I found myself praying that God would do something. If, as the neurologist at the children's hospital said, she was not going to live more than five years, then I wished she would quietly slip away now to avoid the suffering I imagined she was undergoing. If, however, she was going to live beyond that, then I wanted a miracle, an instant cure. What other prayers were there?

Why would I think that dying would be better for Bree than the life she was living? Would she really be a vegetable? I don't know. I was filled with frustration.

Wendy:

Bree's progress was slow. She started raising her head at six months, was doing some minor rolling by her first birthday. It was easier for me to deal with her daily care and a busy home life than with the negative reactions of some friends. Many who had spent a lot of time with is prior to her birth now didn't darken our door. It was difficult to deal with this change in attitude. We had tried from the start to be open and honest about Bree, but many didn't want to hear because they did not know how to react. They chose to stay away. This had one advantage. It showed us who our true friends were. There is nothing like a hard situation to bring out the best in some people... or the worst in others.

The defection of friends was harder for Walter than for me. I was a newcomer to the area, but he had grown up there and theses were his friends from childhood. I had longtime friends who reacted positively to Bree and new ones who had adverse feelings fell by the wayside and were not missed.

My own emotional and spiritual life started to grow in leaps and bounds after Bree's birth. I didn't realize this at the time, I simply felt tremendous pain. The happiest event in my life had just occurred and yet it hurt so much. Alone at night, I spent a great deal of time in what I supposed could be called prayer. I was talking to God out of desperation. There was no one else to listen.

What was I to do? How could I handle this situation? What had I done wrong? I had made mistakes and yet nothing could merit Bree's being hurt like this. Why was God punishing me? I went over my life again and again, After years of feeling separated from God, I became acquainted with him out of necessity. These were nights of tear and anger. I was very angry with God for letting this happen to our child. Then through all the tears and anger, though all the frustrations and questions, there began a very slow spiritual awakening. I had been brought up as a strict Presbyterian; God was to be feared. I remembered my mom saying things like,

"God will strike you down if you say 'darn'." My father was very good at quoting the scriptures though his everyday language was punctuated with J.C. this and J.C. that, not used in any form of praise. I was forced to attend church. My upbringing was not designed to teach me to love God but to fear Him. As I grew older, that didn't make sense.

When one looks around the world and the universe and beyond, it is hard to believe all that happens is just an accident. There has to be a reason for things... even a brain-injured child. It couldn't be one chance in a million. There had to be a reason why Bree chose us for her parents. The world would work perfectly if man did not interfere. All answers had to be out there somewhere.

My first reaction was that I was being punished which was natural enough in light of my upbringing, Fortunately, after Bree's first year, God and I came to a sort of agreement. (Not that one can make deals with God. I know because I had tried every angle.) But we struck this bargain... ha! *Please show me how to help Bree get well. Put people I need to help us and the information I need to know on my path and I will do the work as I am not afraid of hard work.* This route was the only one for me to follow, the only one that offered hope.

The ideal, of course, would be for Bree to be healed instantly. End of story! But that would mean that we had learned nothing. I believe a brain-injured child is born into a family because there is healing needed in the whole family. This includes parents, grandparents, brothers, sisters, uncles, aunts, cousins, and everyone.

Putting Bree in an institution was never an option for me. This child was part of me. She was family. We were the only ones who loved her enough to make sure she had the proper care. I tremble when I think of all the babies and little children who are sent off to an institution because they do not live up to their parents' expectations. I pity the parents who think it is a disgrace to have a child who is not normal. I grieve for the children who are imprisoned and doomed simply because their parents lack the sense of humanity which would enable them to realize the gift they have been given. Jesus said,

"How you treat the least of my brethren, you treat me."

Many were the nights I spent crying and praying, wondering if I was on the right track, doing the right thing for Bree. I felt so alone and my biggest concern was that I might not be caring for her in the right was and that she would die.

Sometimes I recieved help from unexpected places. An example is the time I started giving Bree vitamins. A doctor scared me by suggesting I needed to be careful as the vitamins might be dangerous for her. I may have known more about nutrition than he did, yet it raised doubts in my mind and that night I prayed for an answer of some sort. The next day I had a call from a woman who had been referred to me by someone at the Mentally Retarded Association. She gave me some information about a stimulation program for Bree. She mentioned that she was giving her daughter vitamins, which have helped her.

Instinctively, I had known it was the correct thing to do. All I needed was assurance to follow my instincts. I was to learn that few doctors at that time knew much about nutrition and that only 30 of the 125 medical schools in the United States offered courses in nutrition. These courses were optional and were only three hours long.

Maternal intuition and my strong desire to do what was best for Bree stood me in a good stead as I kept up my search for information. When I discovered something useful, it would sound right, feel right, and look right. I learned to create a positive attitude towards Bree. Attitude, I am sure, plays a huge part not only in survival but in winning.

One of my main frustrations at that time was caused by Bree's seizures because they made me feel so helpless. I knew very little about seizures and I was afraid one might cause her death. This fear was increased by a doctor's comment that,

"Prolonged seizures can cause further brain-damage and even death."

Trying to live as normal a life as possible was difficult. Small events like birthday parties were hard for me. Bree would lie immobile on a rug while other children swarmed all over the place. I wondered whether the other parents realized how easy parenthood was for them. I also wonder if they would ever get the chance to know what the unconditional love is.

Taking pictures... every family had an album and memories. Have you any idea how difficult it is to photograph a brain-injured child so she would look as normal as possible? I would prop Bree on a pillow, make sure her mouth was closed and check that her eyes were wide open so she didn't have the glazed look of the brain-injured. Many of the pictures I could not bear to keep because she looked so hurt in the, despite my efforts. It was rare that I saw Bree as she looked to others, but those pictures showed me how injured she really was. To me, she was, and is, beautiful.

First trip to Gaspe Cabin, five months old (all)

Chapter 4

Six months after Bree's birth, I had an IUD inserted, but sometime during the spring of 1981, I missed my period and panic set it. Caring for Bree plus my other duties took all my energy and I was barely able to cope. How could I manage with another baby? I felt there was no way I could handle that situation.

Another concern! If I was pregnant, what had happened to the IUD? Floating around somewhere inside of me? Walter's reaction was immediate and unemotional. If I was pregnant, then an abortion was the obvious solution. Indeed, I was pregnant. The doctor could not find the IUD, but and X-ray did. I had visions of it becoming embedded in the embryo's head, causing another brain-injured child. The doctor was as calm about it as Walter. Of course there was no alternative but an abortion. I knew that Bree needed one hundred percent of my attention, so it seemed that abortion was the only solution.

I was torn in two and that casual attitude of other mothers at the clinic surprised me. It seemed that some of them used abortion as a form of birth control. For my part, the feeling of guilt was tremendous. I wanted to have more children and if the circumstances had been otherwise, I would have been ecstatic over this second pregnancy.

Weeks passed. I was still bleeding and the IUD was still inside me. The doctor performed a D and C and the IUD was finally removed. It had been embedded in tissue up against the wall of my uterus. Afterwards, the doctor told me that it would never have been a healthy pregnancy. I would have had a miscarriage or a serious infection. Another pregnancy test came back negative. Walter started talking about a vasectomy, but I was opposed to that; I still wanted children later on when Bree was stronger and hoped he would forget the vasectomy idea.

Walter soon had something else to think about. In the Spring he heard about a ski school for sale and he fancied the idea of purchasing it. His reasoning was that I could run the business end from home and he could help when he wasn't working at St. Sauveur. I was reluctant to consider it. I saw it as taking time away from Bree just when I was looking into a stimulation program that demanded a two-year commitment for seven days a week.

Seeing it as the answer to our financial problems, Walter became insistent and I gave up opposing him as it was taking too much energy. In the meantime, we headed for Gaspe for a two-week vacation. Cousins who lived there had a positive attitude towards Bree and this was very supportive. Walter spent every day windsurfing. My parents arrived towards the end of the second week and then I was able to really relax. One night we had a picnic on the beach. I wrapped Bree in a large blanket so she could see her first bonfire. Mom held her and her eyes were the size of quarters as she took in all the action.

Bree had never been baptized and I planned to have this done in New Carlisle where we would be surrounded by relatives. Walter was not interested in participating in religious rituals and so was indifferent about having the baptism, but it was important to me, a sort of recognition of Bree. My Aunt Marge loaned me the christening gown my grandmother Annett had made and used for all her children. Bree would be the first child to use the new christening font in the church.

The congregation at the church in New Carlisle had diminished and was so small that there was no longer a resident minister. Usually student ministers took the services, but by good fortune a minister who had preached there three years earlier was on vacation and he agreed to conduct the service. I had asked if it was acceptable for only one parent to stand up with the child as Walter indicated he did not want to be involved. At the last minute he decided to come along. I left it up to him whether he participated in the ceremony or not. There were only a few people there other than relatives and once more, at the last minute, Walter decided to stand up in the front of the church with Bree and me.

It was a great relief for me to have the ceremony performed. Bree looked so beautiful… little princess in the white lace dress. Although she was over a year old, the dress made for a three-month-old baby fit her.

We returned home refreshed, ready to face the work involved in the ski school. Bree had her measles shot and one week later she had her first grand mal seizure. A short journal entry said it all: "A terrible night, a night I still fear and feel uncomfortable writing about."

Bree had her own little room adjacent to ours, with a connecting door. At about four in the morning I sensed that her breathing was odd and I went to check on her. I had never seen a grand mal attack before but instinctively knew what it was. We had been warned that if one ever occurred, we should get to the hospital as quickly as possible. The implied dangers of a prolonged seizure were further brain damage and the possibility of death. I don't remember much about that night other than driving to Montreal at an unearthly speed. At the hospital, Walter stayed with Bree. I paced the corridors for hours, praying. (That was to be our pattern over the next few years. Walter would stay in the emergency room, keeping an eye on the doctors. I could not bear to watch Bree shaking out of control, staring into space, and being injected with drugs.) I was scared to death. I prayed, I begged, I pleaded. I don't remember what bargains I tried to make with God, but I am sure I promised anything and everything. It was four long hours before Bree stabilized and came back to us.

That first time we stayed in the hospital three days while tests were made and a drug program commenced. Then Walter went back home and I stayed on, planning to sleep in a rocking chair beside Bree's bed. My brother Garth persuaded me to go to his apartment for the night. The next morning I was back in the hospital at six-thirty and found Bree awake. That decided the future. I would not be leaving her again because I didn't want for her to wake up to strangers in a strange place.

I learned a lot from that hospital stay. When Bree was sleeping, I would wander around the neurology ward. I learned that a hospital was no place to leave a brain-injured child if you wanted her to have the best of care. There were children left in wet or soiled diapers for hours because the busy nurses didn't get around to changing them. There were some impatient nurses who easily lost their tempers with theses children because a child might hate to have a tube put down their throat into the stomach.

Off a seldom used corridor was a small black room and curiosity made me look in one day. Five beds, each occupied by a motionless form, were in this eerily quite room. The only nurse who seemed to be looking after these children was a beautiful, older black woman who told me that other nurses did not want to deal with the children in this room. She had been a nurse for nineteen years and it was obvious that this was a vocation for her, not just a job. One of the children had had a strong reaction to a measles shot and was left severely brain-damaged. His father had visited him once, saw what he was like, and never returned. The boy was now twelve-years old... unwanted and unloved because he did not meet his parents' expectations.

The nurse admitted that she should not be telling me these things, but she obviously needed to get them off her chest and she could see how I felt about Bree and that I was the only parent who was there one hundred percent of the time. She confirmed what I had already seen which was that busy nurses didn't always get around to attending to children and in some cases, a nurse's patience wasn't equal to what was required in a hospital setting. She herself would change these children when she could spare the time from her own duties.

I questioned what makes parents' time so valuable they cannot spare some time for their own children, left alone and waiting to die. These children were given to them for a reason. I firmly believe there are no accidents or unlucky events. It's as though God offers these parents a gift, the most precious gift they could have, and they reply by either saying, "Sorry, I don't have the time," or, "Give me another gift. I do not like this one." This reaction is like that of spoiled children who believe that the world owes them a living and that they owe nothing in return. They fail to realize that there are no guarantees, that was you send out will be returned to you. Actually, the only guarantee is that there are no guarantees.

Thomas Jefferson said, "I tremble for all my species when I reflect that God is just." I tremble for all the parents who, over the years, have rejected their brain-injured children. These parents were given the job of caregivers and had the opportunity to love unconditionally, but they turned their backs on their children. God does not make mistakes. We make them. I know of people who dote on their dogs and cats, leaving pages of instructions when they go on vacation, and yet the idea of spending some time with a beautiful little brain-injured child appalls them. Once again, I repeat, "How you treat the least of these my brethren, you treat me."

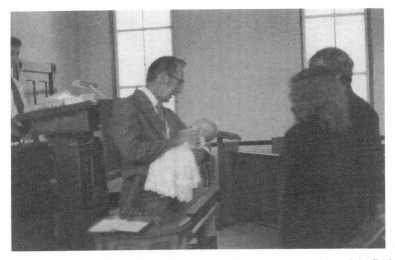

Bree's christening. Bree was 1 year, 5 months old, fitting into a 3-month-old christening dress made by my grandmother.

Chapter 5

In the fall of 81' my Mom sent me a newspaper clipping about a father who was doing a stimulation program at home with his brain-injured daughter. The following week another article arrived from Walter's grandmother about a family in England doing the same program. Both families had learned about his program from a place in Philadelphia. and as soon as I received the second article, I knew I had to contact the people there.

The Institutes for the Achievement of Human Potential sent me a book list and I ordered *What To Do About Your Brain Injured Child*, a book I had heard about and was trying to obtain. Reading it was like having a light go on. These people seemed to be doing something I could sink my teeth into. My prayers were being answered.

I learned from Glenn Doman's book that while the world believes that the parents of brain-injured children are often a problem, he believes they can be the answer to the problem because hurt children can get better and their parents could do the job better than anyone else. The Institutes teaches parents how to work with their children. It believes parents get much better results than professionals do mainly because professionals are taught that injured brains are beyond repair, while parents tend to believe in miracles... and then make them happen.

In his book, Doman explained why he uses the generic term "brain-injured" for all types of deficiency, including mental retardation.

"...The problems are not weak arms or legs or poor musculature, or malformed organs or speech or defective eyes, as much of the world believed, but the problems originated within the brain, out of some accident which occurred before, during, or after birth, and interfered with the brain's ability to respond to it."

This fantastic book was exactly what I had been looking for. All the books I had read in the previous eighteen months had not come close to its principles and ideas. These people at The Institutes were doing things with children that were logical. They believed in these children. They did not believe that simply because they could not walk to talk they were stupid or, at best, not smart. This was so different from what I had encountered so far! It all made so much sense, common sense, that somehow we would have to take Bree to Philadelphia as soon as possible.

This would entail a serious commitment. The parents are required to do a stimulation program seven days a week, including holidays, all day long for a minimum of two years. The mother had to be the major programmer with the father being the second choice. I come from a background believing in a very strong work ethic, so this did not scare me. There was one major obstacle – the eighteen-month waiting list for an appointment at The Institutes – and I sought a way to overcome this.

I wrote a long letter to the Institutes detailing Bree's birth and syndrome and asked for an appointment. Walter, who had read the book, was impressed with the ideas but was hesitant to commit to what this program asked of the parents and he was concerned about the cost. I told him that I had already written to them. I said that we had seen nothing in the year and a half since Bree's birth that even came close to what they proposed. Also, I pointed out that the waiting list was long and that even if we were on it, we could cancel if we wanted to and that if we didn't act now, we would be extending the waiting period. Walter wasn't worried about the length of the wait, but I was deeply concerned because Bree had only been given a possible five-year life span.

March, 1983... that was the date given. Something to look forward to. I sent in the $100 required to confirm the appointment. Walter was concerned about where the rest of the money for visits to Philadelphia and treatment costs would come from. I was serenely sure it would com from somewhere when the time was ripe. March of 1983 seemed an eternity away, but I was full of optimism. I thought of all the professionals I had seen to date, none of whom had made positive changes in Bree. One physical therapist came up with the idea of putting Bree inside an inner tube to teach her how to sit up. I didn't know any better and so I did that for a time. I attended meetings of parent parent groups and found most of the parents were nice, but they had different beliefs. Most had total confidence in the medical profession and were resigned to dealing with doctors and hospitals for the rest of their lives, while I was looking for something different. I didn't know what, but I was determined to keep looking. Maybe it was my growing spiritual beliefs that told me the answers were out there somewhere. Although at that point, I too was very depended on the medical profession and their drug treatments.

Perhaps Philadelphia held the answers. I deeply hoped so!

In the meantime life went on in a series of ups and downs. Bree's first tooth erupted at nineteen months. She had been teething since she was seven months old and suffered considerable pain. By the time she was twenty-months old she had six teeth and she was five and a half before she got a full set. It was a long and painful process. At one stage she screamed for ten straight days. Then a tooth erupted and she was fine… until the next one started to come through. One offshoot of this stress was increased seizure activity, something that happened whenever she was out of sorts. The only thing that gave her any contentment was being rocked in my arms in a rocking chair and I spent days at a time doing that.

God, how I wished I could make it all better. Watching Bree in pain or ill was worse than anything else. I'd run through all the things that might be the cause and when nothing checked out, I'd want to scream, but screaming wouldn't make the problem go away.

Bree was, and is, beautiful to me and it is only when I look back at old picture that I see what an ugly little duckling she really was. She had a big red stain on her forehead, a dazed look in her wide-set eyes, scant hair that refused to grow, and a frightening immobility.

The only times I was aware of how different Bree really looked was when I saw things reflected in the eyes of passers-by who would look at her strangely. I would straighten her up in her stroller, trying to make her look like any other child in a stroller, and then go back to seeing her through my own eyes. One thing I had noticed about other brain-injured children, or pictures of them, was that they always seemed unkempt and disheveled so I made a special point of keeping her dressed nicely, of having everything color coordinated. Some people would comment on her nice outfits and it was true that she did look sweet on them.

Bree taught me a lot about people. She became my gauge for sizing them up. I knew where they stood, first by their reaction to her and then by their conversations with her. Many people said she look sleepy. Another common comment was a question, "What's wrong?" when she did not instantly respond to them. Once Walter's aunt was reading to her and made a mistake. Then she compounded it by saying, "Oh, I made a mistakes, but you wouldn't understand anyway!"

I made a point of keeping people like that away from Bree as much as possible. I was learning so much about life through her. I believe that when people show indifference to Bree, it is because they're afraid. People who tend to believe that a child is stupid if she doesn't respond to them have not caught on to the fact that brain-injured children seek to force them to deal with a higher level of communication… almost a telepathic type of communication. It always surprised me that people that people can understand the needs and wants of their dogs and cats and yet do not realize that with a little extra attention to detail, they could similarly understand the needs of brain-injured children.

The attitude of my family members continued to be one of denial. My father kept saying Bree would grow out of "it" and my mother, so understanding in many ways, was still, a year and a half later, trying to find someone to blame. Once on a visit we were having supper with them and my oldest brother, Ronnie, and his family. Ronnie's attitude was made perfectly clear. He stated in no uncertain terms that he believed mentally retarded children should be "put away". In his opinion, they were useless because they would never be able to do anything.

Dr. Viktor Frankl in his classic book, *Man's Search For Meaning*, talks about usefulness. This book was written about man's freedom to transcend suffering and find a meaning to his life regardless of his circumstances. This came to him during a time he spent as a prisoner in Auschwitz and other concentration camps.

Viktor Frankl wrote,

"Just as life remains potentially meaningful under any conditions, even those which are miserable, so does the value of each and every person stay with him or her, and it does so because it is based on the values that he or she has realized in the past, and is not contingent on the usefulness that he or she may or may not retain in the present.

"More specifically, this usefulness is usually defined in terms of functioning for the benefit of Society. But today's society is characterized by achievement orientation and consequently it adores people who are successful and happy and, in particular, it adores the young. It virtually ignores the value of those who are otherwise, and in doing so blurs the decisive difference between being valuable in the sense of dignity and being valuable in the sense of usefulness."

There I was sitting at the table with my eighteen-month old mentally retarded daughter who was doing nothing. When he realized what he had done, he tried to make an exception of Bree, while my mother tried to smooth the situation over by seeking someone to blame… and I blew up.

I was so tired of their always trying to project blame elsewhere. As if it mattered. Nothing was going to change the fact that Bree was brain-injured. Dealing with the situation as human being was the only answer. I needed support from people, not an endless going around and around in circles.

It's interesting to note that this was the same brother, six years later, who saw Bree clapping her hands and commented on it. I was able to tell him that she had been able to do that for the past five or six years. He had seen her many, many times during that period but had not even noticed. He had not taken the opportunity to learn anything from Bree because he simply did not see her as a person. Later this same brother was to look me straight in the eyes and say that if Bree had been born to him, he would have left her in the hospital! In a way, Bree was invisible to him. I tremble for him.

Another denial situation took place about a month after Bree's first grand mal attack. Walter's job took him away and I went to stay with my parents during his absence. One reason was that if she had another seizure, I needed someone to take us to the hospital. My oldest brother came over with his family, driving his old truck, and my father loaned him his car, so the children could have a more comfortable ride home. That, to me, was bad enough for my father knew I was relying on his car to be available. What made things worse was that he didn't even have the keys to the truck. He thought, rather vaguely, that the keys might be somewhere in the truck itself and became angry with me for panicking when a search showed they weren't there. It was obvious that he was not prepared to face how delicate Bree's hold on life was and how important it was to get a quick medical attention whenever it was needed. In the end, he made a thorough search for the keys and eventually found them.

That night, around midnight, Bree had a seizure, mild enough for her to be out of it before we reached the hospital… but I could shake off the fear of what might have happened had it been a major attack with no transportation readily available.

My father's attitude did not change much over the years that followed. I guess because Bree didn't grow out of "it". she failed to live up to his expectations. But then, I guess he didn't live up to hers either.

When fall came, I put a lot of time into ski school, motivated by the fact that I hoped it would pay for Bree's program in Philadelphia. We hired a friend, Diane Gosselin, to work with me. She had been at the school on St. Sauveur, so we knew it would work out well. There were actually only ten weekends of skiing involved, but these required a lot of preparation. Buses had to be hired, ski hills chosen for the good ticket rates they would give us, and hours had to be spent on the phone getting bookings. We needed a minimum number of children to make it worthwhile. There were two sections of the school, one for older skiers who were taken to a different area each weekend and the other for the youngsters who went to the same ski slope every week. We also had a ladies' day each Wednesday, taking one load of women to a different area each week. The program included ski lessons during the day of skiing and this involved hiring instructors.

A government-funded organization called Service Domicile gave me four hours of help with Bree each week and this allowed me some free time for ski school. One woman who came to the house told me that she had seen another family doing what she believed was the Philadelphia Institutes' program and she promised to get their phone number. This proved to be a lucky break because the mother I contacted said there was a "cancellation waiting list" and if we were in a position to take an appointment on short notice, we could get our name on that list and possibly cut down on our waiting time considerably. The woman was willing to have us visit her home and see the program in action. I arranged to go to her house.

The Hubertoise family lived in a large renovated farmhouse near St. Jerome, about a twenty-five drive south of us. Their son was nine years old and severely brain-injured. Because he was tall and his muscles were very tight, it took five people to pattern him (Patterning is part of the stimulation process that I'll explain later). The father was a partner in a business and was able to take the time off to help his wife with half the patterning program. He looked at Bree and said,

"Ah yes, there is someone in there behind those eyes..."

That was very inspiring to me. He and Walter spent some time together, talking man to man, which gave Walter a better idea of what the program would mean. I took copious notes and, before we left, it was arranged that I could spend a whole day there to see a program from start to finish. The day before I was scheduled to go, Mrs. Hubertoise, Jeanette, called and altered my visit to half a day. I didn't show disappointment but after I hung up the phone, I cried, feeling I might miss something important for Bree in the half-day I wouldn't be there.

Walter's mother looked after Bree when I went, so I could concentrate on what I was learning about the program. I watched, listened, and took notes and Jeanette Hubertoise loaned me three of the Institutes' books. More good information I could use to help Bree. I returned home filled with hope.

The Hubertoise boy was six before his parents found out about the Institutes. Bree was so much younger that she had more of a chance to improve because the younger the child is when the program is begun, the better the results.

There seemed to be a possibility we could get an appointment for the following July. This would suit us perfectly. The ski school would be over and we would have free time. In the meantime I made drastic changes in Bree's environment, making it more stimulating.

Bree motivated me. I could move mountains for her!

4 generation photo: Bree with her father, his mother, and his grandmother.

Chapter 6

Having a successful winter with our ski school became very important because we needed money for the trip to Philadelphia and for the monthly fee that was charged for the program. Walter's mother took care of Bree all day Saturday and Sunday during the ten weeks. This meant extra work for her, as she was also looking after two other grandchildren. She did a great job and I don't know how I could have managed without her help. I would have entrusted Bree to no one else except my mother and as she lived as two-hour drive away, that was out of the question.

The weekends with the ski school were crazy. Walter was kept busy at St. Sauveur, so I was on my own. When the Saturday program was over and the children were on their way home, I was busy with preparation for Sunday activities. If the busses were late because of bad weather or heavy traffic, I would be on the phone for hours consoling parents.

During the day we were all fully occupied running after children, making sure they were happy and, more importantly, that they were all accounted for. Heaven forbid a parent should decide to come collect a child who would not be found instantly. We provided lunches for the whole group that ranged from four to sixteen and food likes and dislikes had to be considered.

It was a six-year old from one of the weekend groups who had yelled,

"Stop acting like a retard!" All I felt was anger. Here I was, stuck with these little rich kids whose parents were happy to get rid of them for a full day and all I wanted was to be home with my own child. She needed me more than these spoiled ones did. Some of the younger children didn't even want to be there. They were only four years old.

They would have preferred to be at home, but their parents were determined to make them great skiers, either that or they just wanted to be rid of them. I did my job teaching them to ski, but I really didn't enjoy it, as I wanted so much to be with Bree. I couldn't understand why parents would send such young children on an hour-long bus ride, to ski all day, and then face the long ride home. Maybe it was a good way to tired a child out.

We survived that first first winter and I paid off quite a bit of the ski school debt (bank loan), all bills and salaries. It was an interesting view of human nature; here were all these wealthy families sending their children to learn to ski, making sure they had the most comfortable busses, the most expensive slopes, and yet many were reluctant to pay for it. They all wanted discounts and special deals… a large group of people who thought the world owed them something.

I planned to do Bree's stimulation program all summer and told Walter not to count on me for our ski school the following winter. I felt certain that by July we would be going to Philadelphia. I cannot explain how I knew this. I just did and told everyone so.

We celebrated the end of the ski season with a party. With a hundred of Walter's ski instructors and their guests, totaled at least two hundred. This would be the last time we would all be together until the following season and we had a sit-down dinner followed by dancing.

There was a surprise for us… a true surprise! At the end of the meal and after the presentation of merit awards, Dave Levy, one of the instructors, stood up to make an announcement that would change many things for us. He said that, without our knowledge, he had been telling people about Bree and our plans.. and he was happy to say that a trust fund holding some $11,000 had been established to pay for all her expenses in Philadelphia.

My financial worries were over. Now, we had money for the trip to Philadelphia and also enough to pay for the two-year program. *Truly,* I thought, *God works in mysterious ways his wonders behold.*

Dave came to the house to give us the details of the trust and told me there was enough to enable me to hire a second person to help with the program. I decided to offer the job to Walter's oldest sister who was not working at the time and she accepted. I gave her *What To Do About Your Brain-Injured Child*, so that she could get an idea of what was ahead of her.

Over the next few months we had Dave over to our house often. We'd invite some other friends as well. It was one way we could show our gratitude. I noticed that he got moody and withdrawn whenever he was not the center of attention. I mentioned this to Walter, but he thought it was perhaps just how he acted when he was tired.

Everything was coming together perfectly. We didn't have to worry about how we were going to pay for the stimulation program and with the ski school finished, I was able to set up a mini-stimulation program for Bree to prepare her for the fall. Walter cut out a wooden alphabet which I used as a stencil to make huge word cards and I started a reading program. Using a design from the Doman book, Walter made an inclined plane so Bree could start a crawling program. This was wonderful as, with the aid of gravity, it gave Bree the idea of what it felt like to be able to move. Fortunately, the six-foot long piece of equipment fitted easily into the large house we were living in at the time.

Daily massages became a part of Bree's program. I wish I had known the benefits earlier as I believe it would have greatly increased her emotional well being had it been used from birth. Now she always gets about an hour massage every day.

Studies have shown that when a baby is held, the heart rate slows, muscles relax, peristaltic waves increase, and digestive juices flow. This holding is crucial to the mother-child bonding. When there is no bonding there are often problems in social bonding later in life. A baby deprived of touching literally shrivels. It is also known that when the digestive juices are not activated, the child fails to receive proper nourishment and its physical growth is retarded.

Monkeys (or brain-injured children, for that matter) when deprived of their mothers show signs of neuroticism and even psychosis. They spent their time sitting passively and staring out into space, with no interest in other monkeys or anything else. How many brain-injured children have you seen doing that?

June 19, 1982:

An absolutely great day! Early that night the Institutes called to offer us a cancellation date for July 19th. Wow, here it was! My only concern was that Walter had responded to the call in an unenthusiastic manner. He told them we would probably accept the opening and would get back to them. I was afraid his response might indicate indifference and give a bad impression. I called back immediately to confirm the appointment, saying that Bree and I would be there one way or another, even if it meant walking! I was so excited that this opportunity had finally come that I spent the rest of the evening dancing around, unable to sit still.

A month till our appointment and, as we might not have a chance for a vacation for the next two years, we decided to spend the last two weeks of that time at the Gaspe cabin.

If we were accepted into the program, there would be a lot of work ahead, but that and the loss of free time seemed a small price to pay to have Bree well. I desperately wanted her to be well. In my prayers I had always told God that hard work was not a problem for me. I just needed to be told what to do.

The Institutes did not guarantee anything, but I knew that even if Bree didn't get totally well, she would be much improved. Only families who are prepared to commit themselves are accepted into the program. This eighteen-month waiting list of families from all over the world who wanted to do the program. Some children die while waiting to get accepted, so why would the Institutes waste time with parents who were not prepared to work seriously at the program to the exclusion of other who would?

I just hoped that when the time came for our interview, Walter would sound as committed as I was. I certainly did not want to be refused a place. All my hopes were riding on this stimulation program.

Chapter 7

Dave Levy was surprised to hear we were getting a July appointment in Philadelphia and when I told him we were having a two-week break at Gaspe, he suggested that we call him on our way back. Then he would have five hundred dollars for us to cover the cost of our trip. The rest of the trust money was tied up in bonds and could not be drawn out on such short notice.

I was hoping to find volunteers at New Carlisle, so I could continue with at least some of the program during the vacation. My cousins Vivian and Carol offered to help, as did Carol's husband Steven who was a distant cousin. They were fantastic and I shall always remember them fondly for their help. They had offered to help without any idea what they were getting themselves in for. Vivian turned up at eight o'clock each morning. Alas, they were the only relative who were willing to help during the entire two and a half years I was doing the program.

Bree was ready for this new stimulation program; the reading part was great fun and the inclined plane worked beautifully in preparing her for a full mobility program. The idea of that apparatus was to get moving any child who had never before moved and therefore had no idea how it felt. Basically, it was a plywood shoot eight feet long and thirty inches wide with eight-inch side boards. The main surface was covered with a smooth sheet of pressed wood. It was raised at one end to a height that would get Bree moving forward with minimal effort on her part. As she became able to travel the entire length, we gradually lowered the height until she was finally flat on the floor and moving without the assistance of the gravity the tilted chute provided. We had been using it for several months before our first visit to Philadelphia and by the time the phone call came offering the early appointment, Bree had just arrived at floor level.

We had high hopes that the Institutes would be the answer to Bree's problems. To date, all the people who had dealt with her had done so in a series of "separate" treatments; eyes, seizures, teeth, and legs were all dealt with independently and by different therapists or doctors. The Institutes' basic principle was that all these different problems were symptoms only and the real cause of them was the brain itself and therefore it was the brain that should be treated instead of individual parts of the body.

The drive to Philadelphia was dreadful. It was during a heat wave and we didn't have air conditioning in the car. Each time we stopped for gas or food, I took Bree to the restroom and gave her a sink bath to cool her off. We did the eleven-hour drive in a single stretch and were very tired by the time we reached our hotel. The dining room was air-conditioned and when we went for supper, Bree was soon fast asleep in the booth.

That night the air-conditioner in our room was not working properly, so we had a fitful sleep. That was unfortunate because we had been warned ahead of time that the first day at the Institutes would be a twelve-hour one. They were not exaggerating. After an initial meeting with Glenn Doman, we were taken in hand by Lee Pattinson who began what was to be a very bulky file on Bree by taking down a detailed family history. We then went on to see other people, all doing different testing to assess Bree's abilities and deficiencies. We saw the last one at one a.m. and the last at 2:45 a.m. I was most impressed. I had never seen professionals so dedicated to their work and it was obvious that people putting in that sort of hours had to love brain-injured children.

At our last interview on that first day, we were told Bree was a candidate for the Institutes' program. It sometimes happens that some children who come have been misdiagnosed and are not brain-injured but have psychotic or other problems which the Institutes does not deal with. In a way it was rather odd to feel relief at being told your child was brain-injured and a strange twist to realize that if she had not been, she would not have been accepted for the problem.

There was still no certainty that we would be accepted and we wouldn't know that until the end of the week, after several more interviews. As I explained earlier, because of the long waiting list, the Institutes goes to great length to ensure that parents understand what is demanded of them and are willing and able to do a full program with their child. Otherwise, they would be politely but firmly rejected and another family would be given the opportunity.

We spent all of Tuesday, Wednesday, and Thursday in the lecture auditorium. I found it very hard to leave Bree with strangers. I knew the lectures were an important part of our learning process but I worried about being away from her a full day. Walter couldn't understand my deep concern that was caused by fear that a problem might occur and I would not be there. The children were cared for by the same staff members we had already seen who, in addition to caring for their physical needs, also took the opportunity to discuss each child and begin preparing programs to suit individual needs.

The three days of lectures were fantastic. We were in our seats for a s total of ten to twelve hours each day. The lectures lasted fifty minutes and then there were ten minute breaks and a short-lunch period. The auditorium itself was kept at a below-average temperature, the result of NASA studies that showed that intelligence and alertness are heightened by cooler temperatures. We needed to be totally alert because there was so much information to be absorbed.

Glenn Doman was the principal speaker and he spoke each morning for a full period, lecturing without notes as he taught the beginning of child brain development, as the bae we would be using for the treatment of our children. Much of the material was from his book, What To Do About Your Brain-Injured Child, and the lecture period gave him an opportunity to expand beyond the limitations set by the size of his book. As well as outlining many of the successes of families on the program, he also gave details of many studies and experiments that had been done elsewhere in the world and the results achieved. What he said just made sense: plain common sense. One aspect that he strongly emphasized was the need for positive attitudes an unconditional love being demonstrated by any family hoping to improve the condition of their brain-injured child.

Friday was D-day for the families. This is when they would ding out if they had been accepted for a program and, is so, they would be taught one specifically designed for their family.

During the three days that the staff had taken care of her, Bree had been evaluated and at the Friday interview we were told she tested at an eight-month level of ability. She was twenty-seven months old. She was tested higher than her medical history suggested. This was because I had already started the program at home and so she was recognizing words and therefore tested higher on the visual and intellectual levels. Because of the work on the inclined plain, she tested higher on the mobility level. Altogether she had been tested on six levels: visual, auditory, tactility, mobility, language, and manual competence. These were the six levels which the Institutes, after forty years of studying man and his development, had identified as the six functions that characterize humans and distinguish them from other living creatures. All are unique and all are functions of his cerebral cortex.

The Institutes had also identified them as the six things that are life's test of intelligence and that each of them occurs in the seven vital stages of the brain's development, beginning at birth and ending at six years of age. They also discovered that excellence in these suc levels is not inherited but acquired, and it is possible to improve all of them by selective programs. Because they are interrelated and dependent on each other, improvement in one of these abilities had an effect on all of the others. For example, it is not possible to to improve a child's mobility without also improving visual, manual, auditory, and tactile ability.

The Institutes had designed a Profile on which to record each child's competence level, so that a look at this would show exactly where the child's ability lay in relation to each function, and which areas needed concentrated attention. The Profile done for each child at the initial visit is updated on successive visits, so that a complete record of neurological development is shown.

The news that we had been accepted for a program brought mixed reactions. On the one hand, there stretched two years of hard work. On the other hand, this was our daughter's life and why would we not be willing to give that time to her? As Bree had developed a habit of rolling onto her back on the floor and then staying in that position, we were shown how to make an anti-roll device. Rolling does nothing to advance the mobility of a child and in fact is "surrender" position of an animal. To move forward, a child must be in the prone (face down) position, so that the arms and legs will propel the body forward as they move. We were given a "patterning" program in which the arms and legs of an immobile child are moved in what would be the natural movements of a crawling child, so that the brain learns how these movements feel. A pattern is established that a child can put to use independently.

We were also told that Bree was to be a "floor" baby, which meant she would spend most of a twenty-four hour day on a safe, clean, warm floor (facing downwards) so as to give her the maximum opportunity to move. The idea was the the greater the amount of movement Bree acquired, the more purposeful her crawling would become, and the sooner she would acquire the necessary strength and balance to be able to get up on hands and knees and creep. This would be the initial step that would lead to standing and walking. Massage would send in tactile messages, her reading program would continue, giving auditory and visual stimulation, and her nutritional program would include vitamins.

After having been taught the program, we were surprised to be told that we were not to decide on the spot whether or not we would actually undertake to do it. The Institutes suggested we return home and discuss it, especially with any family members who might be involved in the program or affected by it, and then, away from the enthusiasm of the staff in Philadelphia, make a sober and reasoned decision about what we had been told and taught. If we decided to go ahead with the program, we would return at regular interval to have Bree re-evaluated and, as necessary, have a new or additional program designed for her.

One service provided by the Institutes that we had not seen elsewhere was their Advocate system. Under this, a specific member of the staff was given the responsibility of several families with whom he or she was expected to keep in touch. This meant that the Advocate knew the child and the parents intimately and was totally conversant with the program that was being followed in all its aspects. It also meant that a family having problems could call an individual directly to discuss possible solutions. What a difference this is from other organizations. If you call a hospital about a child who has been treated there, you are not likely to find anyone who remembers any details or is at all familiar with that particular child. My experience had been that a child becomes a number in a file and it is necessary for someone to look up a chart to learn what happened at the last visit.

There had been twenty-seven families in our group and these included the best fathers I have seen. I have expected to meet caring mothers, but the fathers were right in there too, taking responsibility as well. I hoped that this had been a good opportunity for Walter to talk with other fathers who were in the same situation as he was.

On our last day of lectures, we were told the odds were that three would not be accepted as suitable for the program. One family would decide against taking on the work and so would not return. Two children would show little or no improvement. Twenty-one children would improve, ranging from showing significant improvement to becoming totally well. How badly I wanted to be in this last group.

Anti-roll device (left) Anti-sit device (right)

Inclined plane (above)
Patterning (below)

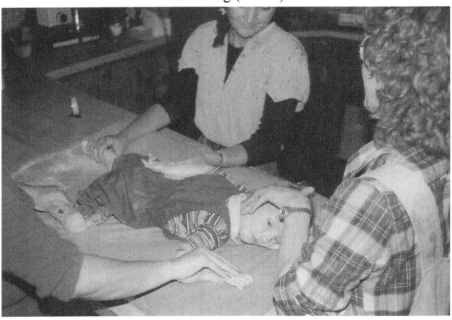

Crawl box to keep Bree from lunging

Teaching reading words (above)
Creeping over obstacles (below)

Living room full of handmade equipment by Bree's dad (above)
Beginning crawler (below)

Walking under overhead ladder (above)
Vestibular equipment (below)

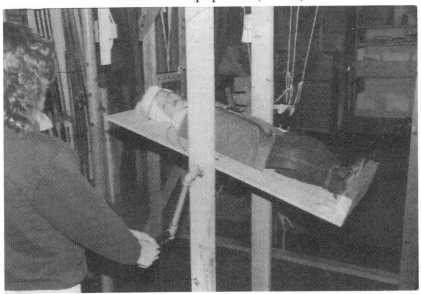

Getting to be a good, little creeper

All of the information put together by the volunteers that were shown to Bree

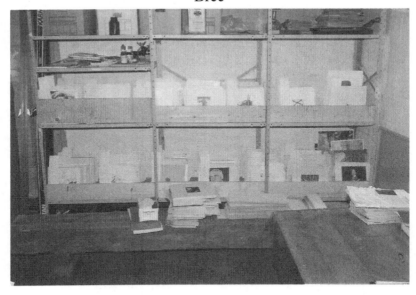

Quad-positioning to strengthen Bree to become a creeper (She loved this!)(above)

Sample of information we made for Bree

Chapter 8

The drive home was long and exhausting. Bree had the beginnings of a cold and her teeth were bothering her. We were all tired and badly needed to catch up on sleep.

I had no intention of doing what the Institutes had suggested, waiting two weeks to decide whether we were going to do the program. I was all set the next day to start preparations for it. Bree was accustomed to the mini-program I had begun and I had things like reading words already prepared. What I needed most were volunteers to pattern her, because called for three people at a time. Each patterning session lasted five minutes and we were scheduled to do twelve a day, with a minimum of twenty minutes between each session.

Somehow I sensed the people would come.

Two days later the patterning program was underway. Walter's sister Sco came four days a week, so we needed only one other patterner for the other days. Service Domicile was able to provide someone twice a week, so it was all coming together quite quickly.

It was important to have a full roster, to cover emergencies, so I set about looking for other helpers. I noticed the house across the way had been rented and, made bold by desperation, I crossed over to find out it a new neighbor might be willing to fill in until we had a suitable full-time local group. I was fortunate. Not only were the newcomers willing to help, but present at the time of my visit was a local woman named Annette Lafromboise who became a most consistent patterner and a close friend and my first spiritual guide. She was the one who was always there to hill in if someone else had to cancel and leave me one helper short. Not until much later did I learn that the two renters were actually nuns on vacation. Annette was a born again Christian and had been for four years at that stage.

My own spiritually was very basic, definately at the infant stage, and there was still quite a struggle going on between me and God. I was very much afflicted by the "Why me?" syndrome. It consisted primarily of a belief in God and the sending out of a lot prayers motivated by my desperation to keep Bree alive and to heal her as quickly as possible. I believe that at this point I still feared God and saw Him in the role of a disciplining father.

Another angel appeared – I do not remember how Andrianne Jackson found out about what we were doing but she volunteered to help and to find other helpers, too. She worked as a volunteer at the local library and quickly picked up on the type of person we needed, so that the patterning schedule was soon filled by a wonderful group of people, women I would never have come to know if it hadn't been for Bree. Their age ranged from forty to seventy, most with children grown and away from home. In total, we had twenty-five women, some coming once a week for two hours, others every two or three weeks and the majority stayed with the program for the entire two and a half weeks and the majority stayed with the program for the entire two and a half years that I did it. Only one major snowstorm kept them away, which was amazing to anyone who knew the road up to our house. It was a winding country road with sharp turns and all uphill for the whole five minutes from the village.

I could not help contrasting the willingness of these volunteers with the reluctance to be involved that was displayed by most of our relatives. My mother-in-law, when I praised the patterners, proposed they did it simply because they got something out of it. It made them look good and satisfied their egos. I didn't believe that for a moment.

These volunteers were my main contact with the outside world for the two and a half years and it was a great learning experience for me. Never had I interacted with a group of women this size and certainly never with ones over the age of forty.

Normally, the Service Domicile aids the housebound elderly, but in my case, an exception was made. I was given four hours a week of aid. The two women who shared the chores stayed for the whole period. Both were French Canadians and spoke very little English, which was good for me because it helped maintain my French and meant that while they were there, Bree only heard French as her second Language. They were not directly involved with her program, but undertook household jobs such as vacuuming and cleaning. Getting the stimulation program done properly occupied all my time and left no time for even thinking about cooking, laundry, and cleaning.

Bree's daily program consisted of eleven patterning sessions. She spent four hours on the floor to improve her mobility. There were eighty-nine "maskings," of one minute each as part of a respiratory program. Children who do not move around much have difficulty increasing lung capacity. Masking is a method developed by the Institutes to counteract this problem. A specially designed plastic bag was placed over Bree's nose and mouth. At the end of the bag is a tube to breath through. In order to get enough oxygen into the lungs, Bree was forced to take deep breaths and this helped develope her lungs. To improve tactility, her skin was stroked and brushed and massage was administered. Lights and horns were used to stimulate visual and auditory pathways, and there was her intelligence program.

The tactility program was one of the more visible successes. Prior to it, I could have tickled Bree for hours without getting any response. Several sessions of brushing and scrubbing were done daily, the idea being that once she was responding enough to indicate a dislike for having it done, we had made the breakthrough we sought. She became fully aware of touch, an awareness that had previously been absent.

Reading was regarded as a reward and was fun at the end of one of the sessions. There were some people who were surprised at the idea of so young a child being able to read, but why not? After all, we are not surprised when a baby who has listened to a mother and others since birth is able to talk. The baby has had the oral stimulation that teaches words and their meaning. Why should there not be visual stimulation that does the same thing? First the child learns what the words look like, then learns to connect them in sentences, exactly the same way he does when he learns to talk. One of the main reasons why small children have not learned to read earlier, the Institutes believes, is that print has been too small for their immature sight. Enlarge the print and show the words often enough, and the battle is won.

So, we were teaching our little brain-injured child to read as the first step on the ladder of human intelligence. The requirements were the ability to take in information, the ability to store it, the ability to retrieve it, and then the ability to combine and permute the information and use it to solve problems.

At firsts the response to the auditory and visual stimulation part of the program was absolutely nil. We had a box made with a plexiglas top, with lights totaling one thousand watts installed, as well as a loud horn that sounded each time the lights were switched on. The noise the horn made was so loud that I wore industrial ear protectors, but was astonished to see that there was absolutely no reaction from Bree. The purpose of the program was to stimulate the visual pathways (the wattage was prescribed depending on the degree of lack of vision of the individual child) and the horn going off at the same time was to form an association in the child's mind. A normal child of Bree's age would have had strong startle reflex when the horn sounded. As with the tactile program, the idea is to continue until the child responds in the normal manner one might expect, then you know you have achieved the response sought and the sessions cease.

The mobility program was a mountain to climb. It takes an enormous amount of effort for an immobile child to move even an inch or two and when I look at videotapes of Bree in those early years, I am overcome by the determination she showed trying to move herself forward. She would literally heave herself up on her arms and fling herself forward, then repeat the action again and again. The motivation for this tremendous action was provided by me. I would sit a short distance from her and call her to come to me. Looking at the effort she put into doing this made me realize just how much she wanted to be close to me. I have seen many adults abandon a task when they met up with the slightest resistance. I have also watched little brain-injured children struggle against all sorts of physical handicaps to move across a room to a waiting parent, knowing that the parent was the one person who loved them unconditionally, more than life itself!

But Bree didn't make any progress that first day. She spent all her effort trying to get rid of her anti-roll device so she could get over in her back. She looked at me, bitched and complained, and then moved forward not a single inch. The second day she traveled thirteen and a half feet in the four hours allotted to her mobility session. By the fifth day she had gotten the message that this was going to be a regular part of her program, accepting it as such, and began to move. That fifth day she traveled more than fifty feet.

One of the things that Walter's sister Sco did that helped me was to prepare the entire reading program, which freed me to attend to other parts of the intelligence program. In the evenings when Bree was asleep, I caught up on what jobs I could that the Domicile Service hadn't done: extra laundry, some house cleaning, and more like that.

Excerpts from a journal I kept for a short period (August 12th to September 26th, 1982) give some idea of what life was like in those days.

August 12th:

Bree has only slept two full nights in about three weeks. This sort of thing I find wears me down. One of her front teeth is pushing through with another one. She has had a cold now for three weeks. When Bree is sick, I'm not in a good mood. I get frustrated as I do not know what to do and I worry about the program. What if she does not get well? When I called Philadelphia about Bree's cold and a rash on her chin, I found out that a little boy in our group who had some down with pneumonia died on the following day, July 26th. Our children are so fragile, with so many odds to overcome, with death knocking at the door. My heart goes out to this family. It could so easily have been us.

Bree has been in a bitching mood for a couple of days now and it wears me down. I am still scared that this all might not work. Whenever Bree is sick or feeling off, she responds less and this is very depressing and scary. Is she slipping away? I find it hard to keep myself up and positive. I prayed that I could hold it all together. I was feeling tired doing the program. Walter and I have barely had any time together. Money is very tight. Dave Levy is not coming through with the money. We had to pay Sco $100 from our own money, which we can't afford. Supposedly, there is money for Bree but it is all tied up and I found myself in the position of having to call Dave about bills to be paid. I hate this. I feel like I am always begging for money. I wish we had enough to pay for all her needs on our own. Being tired and feeling depressed about money and Bree being sick. It is not a good day.

August 13th:

Bree did ten feet each session on the floor today. The teeth are a major problem right now. She always seems to be bothered by teeth. It is a pain. Tonight I went to the health food store and bought rolled oats, bulgar, long grain brown rice, and bran with plans of making a really good hot cereal. Got out of the house to go food shopping for an hour and a half.

August 15th:

Bree did one hundred and sixty feet today. Another tooth through… that makes seven. Went to a party with friends and got fed up with their attitudes. They're always indicating I will burn myself out and asking what about our marriage. No one seems to support us. All they do is criticize. Others who were invited to come and see for themselves what we were doing just didn't turn up as it was arranged. As to whether Walter and I will make it through this… well, either we will or we won't and I'm not going to sit around worrying about is. Bree, the program, and the reaction of friends and family got me back to God. My spiritual life has been on hold for a long time. I felt there was no one on our side but God and Mom. Walter and I have our problems because of not having money, Whenever we quarrel, it is about the lack of money and not knowing how we are going to pay our bills. This situation, if both people involved are willing, could make us stronger. I know what is important… saving our daughter's life.

August 17th:

Sco has just reminded me of things we have noticed about Bree. Her general awareness is much better, her hair is growing faster, there is muscle tone in her arms and legs, and she is grabbing things with strength, like a hard pinch. When we are patterning her, she will sometimes move on her own. Bree did very well today. One floor section she finished in two minutes, which is excellent. The only thing I am finding out is that I do not have any time for myself.

August 18th:

Today Bree's grandmother Scofield and her great-grandmother Scharf came to see the program. Grandmother did the last patterning with us and Bree did something new. She gave her grandmother a hard time, but she was laughing and smiling as though it was a joke. Usually when she is giving us a hard time, she is on the verge of tears. When it came time for the floor session, I proposed letting her sit in grandmother's lap as a reward. She easily did the exercise in two minutes to get this reward. She did one hundred and ninety-two feet today. She is easily distracted now, looks around at everything.

August 24th:

Bree is teething, not doing so well. She moved only thirteen feet on the floor at a session. She was making lots of sounds, also got up on all fours but could not figure out what to do with her hands. It felt like it was a toss up between whether she would say her first word or creep for the first time. I get scared that she might plateau out. I hope that I am not lying to myself about things I am seeing. She still has a cold and I cannot figure out why. Finished program at 7 p.m. and prepared her vitamins for tomorrow. Sco prepares Bree's food as long as I have ingredients ready. I think most other husbands on the program help out more. The program is great for giving me something solid to work with. What is frustrating is when Bree has a cold or is teething. I feel like my hands are tied, feel so totally helpless. I needed a patterner. I knew my brother Richard was visiting his in-laws nearby and I called to ask him if he would help out. His reaction was to ask,

"Where's Walter?" All these wonderful strangers coming to help and my family feels they are being imposed upon. In a way, they are afraid of Bree and they don't even realize that they are. What surprised me is that people will choose to remain ignorant when they are given an opportunity to learn love and compassion. Reactions of family and friends has really surprised me... disappointed me. There are times when I feel that Bree's brain-injury is peeling from her like the skin from an onion. Sometimes when she is lying on the floor I see her move her hands and arms in the way that we pattern herm as though the connection is being made in her brain.

August 30th:

My birthday, 10:30 p.m. and Bree is still awake and crying. I have given her antibiotics, aspirin, and milk... and she still screams. This is driving me crazy. Will her teething ever be over? Walter is talking to her. Will probably have to take her into bed with us. Aside from teeth, she is doing quite well, putting on weight. She doesn't need her anti-roll device any more.

My cousin Valerie came visiting from the Gaspe coast. Breakthrough with Bree today... she crawled to where I was sitting at the table and when I put her back across the room, she crawled over to me again. This is the first time she has done that.

September 14th:

Bree is doing very well. She is moving around a lot now and gets frustrated if she runs into obstacles like bookcases. Went to a corn roast. Took a picture of Bree solo on a toy horse, the first time she has ever sat up without being propped, so it is a rather special photo. One of the people at the party commented,

"Well I never thought she'd get that far." That hurt, but at least is was honest. Bree did a 360° turn today for the first time, crawling right around the island of bookshelves in the middle of the room.

September 17th:

A patterner came in last Tuesday with a cold and now I have one and Bree and Walter are feeling off. I wish patterners understood that it is better off to miss a day than come with an infection. I fell apart when Bree gets sick. We haven't been able to do a decent program for days.

September 25th:

Bree did about twenty-five feet of movement for her Dad today and he was very happy. A friend of his has offered to do a video of her, so we'll have a record of her progress. We need a better crawling environment for her. I asked Dave to look into getting a rug for her to crawl on.

September 26th:

Bree is up to five hundred and twenty-six feet of movement a day. Small seizure two Sundays ago; called Philadelphia and they advised masking, which worked. Her mobility has been at a standstill now for about two weeks, but the Institutes said not to be concerned as she has already passed the goals set for her this period. They suggested that I tie her rewards to the time she takes to complete a session, giving her more reasons for going faster. It worked and two days later she was off on her way again.

These journal references give some idea of what life was like for two and a half years. I also did some taping and when I listen to the tapes again, I get a very strange feeling. I sound so tired, lonely, and scared… afraid I might not succeed, knowing that for failure I would pay a very high price, the life of a child. Pain and fear resound through those tapes and I cry when I listen to them. I don't know why I have kept the journal and the tapes but it is good as it brings home to me how deep that fear and pain were. I was frightened mother trying to figure out how to keep her child alive and healthy.

I had thought that Sco might like to accompany us on a revisit to the Institutes. She could sit in on the lectures and see the wonderful work that was being done. I was wrong. She was not interested. She was getting to be very uptight and I never knew what sort of mood she would be in when she arrived each day. I needed a revisit to meet up with other parents and get feedback from the staff. Dave said his mother was getting together some people to raise money to do program until Bree starts school and he was talking of holding a black-tie fundraising dinner when we returned from Philadelphia. Dealing with the stimulation program and everything else was very stressful, and whenever Bree was off-color, the stress went over the top for me. Whatever was bothering Sco was too much for me to deal with. I had to focus all my attention on Bree. The only thing that kept me together was prayer. I depended on God to work things out.

Sco lost interest and stopped doing the reading program in the middle of October and I had to ask her not to return because her mood swings were too hard for me to cope with and were affecting the whole family. Annette took over. Walter's mother called when she learned that Sco was not coming back and asked me to take her back, saying if I did not, we would be cut off from Walter's whole family. When I explained that it was not working out, Sco took over the conversation and told me that Bree was the result of bad karma… that we deserved her.

My whole body started shaking and I could not stop. I hung up, unable to believe that Sco was thinking that way. How could she have worked with Bree for so many months and have that attitude? I had been heading out the door to do some shopping and I cried all the way to the village. How could anyone say something so hateful about our little girl?

Walter was very upset about it. I knew that now I would have to deal with rejection from his family, but Bree was my priority and it seemed as though rejection was part of the path we were treading.

Chapter 9

We were back in Philadelphia and I optimistically expected Bree to show great gains, perhaps as much as ten months neurological. I was very disappointed. The results showed only a two-month gain after three-and-a-half month program. My optimism was the result of not understanding what counted as gains and what did not. Only things that would help advance a child to the next level of development were given credit. For instance, sitting better was not going to make Bree a walker, whereas creeping and crawling would. So creeping and crawling were a plus... sitting didn't count. I understood this when it was explained to me, but it didn't help ease my disappointment and I went outside and cried, wondering if Bree would ever catch on... and if I would be able to survive until she did.

Despite this setback, we had a great time renewing acquaintances with other families. We knew they were all going through the same difficulties that we were. We had another couple of days of lectures and were given an even more intensive program for the following months.

Our visit was marred by one shocking disclosure. I was asked to stop by the account office and a very pleasant young woman politely asked how we planned to deal with our payments for Bree's stimulation program. I didn't understand. Dave had asked that the bills be sent directly to him, to be paid out of the trust fund. The bills had not been paid. The woman was very understanding, suggesting that I check out what was happening and then get back to the,. I hurried off to find Walter and tell him what had happened.

I reached Dave by phone and was even more worried by his evasive manner. He eventually said the money in the trust was tied up till February, but everything could be paid off then. Embarrassed and feeling ashamed, I returned to the account office and this time asked if all bills could be sent to us, so that we would know what was being paid and what was not.

As soon as we returned from Philadelphia, I phoned Dave again and he said he would send a check for the total amount owed, but it took a couple more phone calls before the check arrived... in December. We deposited it, but feeling nervous, waited for it to be cleared before sending off our own check to Philadelphia. That turned out to be a good move as Dave's check came back marked NSK. The bank told me there was no money in that particular account, nor had there been for some time. Something was seriously wrong. I didn't want to bring Dave's family into this situation but I felt I could do nothing else. When I called his mother, I learned that not only did he have no money, but that his family had been having other problems with him.

I was stunned by the end of the conversation. Not only was there no trust fund, but there never had been. What money he had paid out for Sco's wages and our original trip to Philadelphia must have come from donations he had received from friends who believed there would be a fund. The trust fund was a figment on Dave's imagination.

Some indications of what might have been behind his actions came when his mother told me Dave had shown her a video of Bree and told her that what I was doing for Bree was an example of a mother's true love. Obviously there were currents of resentment running deep and dark there. We will probably never know the full story behind what went on.

What stunned me the most was that Dave had used the plight of a brain-injured child to bolster his own ego. He had been a hero on the night of the ski school party when he announced the existence of the trust fund. My first reaction, after I recovered from the initial shock, was one of blind anger. Not because of the missing money, but because this person had been a welcome guest in our house and had used our little daughter for his own selfish ends. If I never saw him again, it would be too soon... and I could not predict how I would react if I did.

None of that changed the situation. We were $2000 in debt to the Institutes and had to figure out how to pay it. Walter was pessimistic about our prospect of any further trips to Philadelphia. We had, of course, incurred additional expense by hiring Sco, which we would not have done if we hadn't thought the money was going to be available. My response was that we would keep on doing the program till January and have faith that the money would appear from somewhere for our scheduled trip back to Philadelphia that month.

The pace was hectic. Patterners were in and out of the house all day and I was busy from 7 a.m. till 10 or 11 at night. Diane was running the travelling ski school from our house and Walter was still at Mount St. Sauveur. The plan was that Walter would help Diane out by recruiting pupils by phone at night. This is what I had done the first year, but Walter would not do it and the result was the school was slipping away. We were not filling the busses and thus were losing money. I couldn't worry about it. I had enough to do without trying to keep Walter up on his responsibilities.

Our scheduled revisit to Philadelphia had been set for January 16, 1983. We knew ahead of time that even if we raised the money to go, Walter would not be able to get away as that is the busiest part of the ski season. I asked Annette LaFramboise if she could accompany us and she agreed. Now I had to raise some extra cash to cover the expense of the trip. I had no idea where the money was going to come from.

I had one asset, a set of skis that had only been used eight times and were worth at least $300. I decided to sell them even though they were the first new skis I ever had. I didn't know if I would ever ski downhill again. If I did, I wanted Bree by my side.

The money from the sale made the trip possible. The trip was very draining. I felt more tired than I ever remembered being. Annette's company was great, but the responsibility for Bree was totally mine. However, as usual, meeting the other families again was fantastic and it was inspiring to be there for the lectures and learning a new program for Bree.

The day we were to return home, twenty-nine inches of snow fell – breaking a century-old record. Being Canadians, such a snowfall did not perturb us, but the Philadelphians sure had problems coping with it. We were snowed in at the motel and had to dig our way out. The motel owner was surprised to see us doing it. He was from India and snow was another world for him. He put out plastic bags over his shoes to come outside. We all laughed, watching him slipping and sliding all over the place. He was no help in getting us unstuck, but our mutual laughter was a moral booster.

We were faced with an eleven hour drive home and it seemed we were the only people who managed to get moving. We saw some of the other Institutes' dads shoveling snow as were passed the Holiday Inn. These families were from Texas and this must have been a totally new experience for them.

Once we got on the freeway heading north past New York City we had clear lanes all the way. The only other cars we saw were those abandoned by the sides of the highway. It was the easiest drive I had ever had... no traffic and a beautiful day with clear blue skies and a blanket of clear white snow covering up everything. It looked so picture perfect, not the impression one usually gets on a drive between Philadelphia and New York.

The first year of programming was also the beginning of my spiritual growth on a conscious level. Annette was, in one way, my first spiritual guide. We had a lot of time to talk during the patterning and she patiently answered all my questions. What I was experiencing was not the fire and brimstone type of religion I had learned as a child, with a God who punished and was to be feared. I began to experience a God who loved unconditionally and with unlimited understanding and patience. I found a Christian bookstore in Montreal and began to read anything I could find on Healing. The first books I bought were by people I had never heard about: Catherine Marshall, Agnes Sanford, Frances McNutt, Thomas Merton, and Corrie Ten Boom. It was a whole new world opening up with unlimited possibilities.

Annette told me about healing services that were being held in some Roman Catholic churches and we arranged to take Bree to one in Montreal. It would be great to say that a miracle occurred, but that was not the case. I felt I had nothing to lose by believing and hoping. Why not hope? There are no benefits to be gained by hopelessness. Annette was far more advanced spiritually than I was and she was a great help in my search for answers. Bree got an earful of spiritual talk during the patterning sessions.

We had been doing the programming for almost ten months and Bree was progressing well. There were still delays because of teething problems and I continued to live in fear of her having another grand mal attack. We had Bree sleeping in our room as that was the only way I could get a decent night's sleep. She had always had her main seizures during the night and this meant I would check on her frequently during the night. When she was beside me, I could sleep soundly, knowing I would hear her if she began to have a seizure. The Institutes had started Bree on a detoxification program in hopes of weaning her off the seizure drugs she was taking, but she always had to be put back on them. Teething caused her a great stress and pain. Whenever a tooth was erupting, Bree's response would be more seizure activity.

Financially we were in a deep hole. We still owed the original $2000 to the Institutes and the program charge was $300 monthly in US money (At the time the exchange rate with Canadian money was 35%). They travelling ski school was not doing well at all and it looked as though we might not get through the season and then have to declare bankruptcy. We had a bank loan to pay off and had our house on the market to raise cash, but the real estate in Quebec at the time was an all-time low. We had lots of lookers but no buyers.

The community knew of the difficulties we were having. The Boy Scouts raised $1100 through a bottle drive and the Mt. St. Sauveur ski school raffled off a pair of skis and raised $750. All the money was sent directly to the Institutes. The women of the Roman Catholic and Protestant churches decided to combine forces and hold a bake sale.

About this time and article which made me angry appeared in the Montreal Gazette. It stated there was no hope for the mentally retarded. I suggested that they should come to our house and learn what could be done. They arrived, took notes and pictures, and we saw Bree on the center of the front page, walking under her overhead ladder.

The article, full of hope and inspiration, was surrounded by the regular depressing stories about death and war and disagreements of all sorts. The title of the article was "Young Determination And A Mother's Love." It must have given many people to think about. The result was that we were given donations from newspaper readers and we received a call from the manufacturer of UFO Jeans, maker of clothes for children. Bree had been had been wearing a pair of their jeans and they called to ask for her size, saying they would send $200 worth of clothing.

It was nice to think about how Bree was uniting so many people in a common cause, yet it was difficult for me to adjust to getting help and donations. I had been taught to work for my money and not to impose on others. However, it is amazing what one will do when it means saving one's child. We needed all the help we could get and there was no room for the pride here. Walter was working, but I couldn't take a job because doing the programming took one hundred percent of my time. We gladly accepted the aid offered and were grateful for it. Without help we would not have been able to continue for the two and a half years required.

Walter would sweat over bills, getting into a terrible mood each month when they arrived. I believed that somehow God would provide what we needed and I would point out how things had worked in the past. It was harder for him to cope because as a child he'd had everything he wanted materially. He'd had a much easier life than me financially than mine. He was unable to deal with just letting things go and believing that as long as you were putting all your effort into something, things would work out. Providence would step in.

I became an expert at finding clothing at discount prices, always buying at the end of a season and rarely paying full price for anything. Bree always came first. It is normal, I believe, for a mother to put her child first... that was the way my seventy-year-old mother had done ever since her first child was born.

Chapter 10

April, and time for another Institutes revisit, but this time there was a difference. A friend, Gilles Daze, asked where we stayed when we went to Philadelphia. When he heard it was in a motel, he arranged for us to have the use of an apartment belonging to a friend of his who rarely used his place, having a second home in the mountains. This was a fantastic break for us. The friend, Mike McGinn, refused to accept any payment. This saved us a great deal of money, an important factor as during this stressful period we were using our credit cards to limit paying off only the minimum each month as we were living paycheck to paycheck. In addition to that welcome aspect, staying in an apartment was much more comfortable. I had a kitchen, so preparing Bree's food was much simpler and she could sleep soundly in the bedroom while Walter and I were in the living room. This was a huge change from having only one room and having to be as quiet as possible when Bree was asleep.

How things always seemed to work out, even at the eleventh hour! Somehow things always seemed to work out no matter how scary or threatening the situation was.

I always welcomed our revisits, both as a break from the routine of doing non-stop patterning and as an opportunity to share experiences with other mothers. About ten of the families who were in our original group had become very close and we began a habit of going to dinner together once during our revisit time. An interesting evening: ten couples with their brain-injured children. We always selected a good restaurant and we certainly created an impressive impression wherever we went. It must have seemed unusual to see our kids on chairs, in highchairs, or sleeping in little carry-alls under the table… all little hurt children, yet we were just having a good time like any other group of friends with their children.

The knowledge that other mothers in all parts of the world were daily doing a program similar to ours got me through many a difficult day, though as far as I was concerned, doing the program was the only choice I had because it was the only option that presented itself. I was not prepared to accept the prognosis given by some doctors that Bree had no future. 4P- is so rare that little was known about it, except that children with the problem had a short life span. I had to find a way to make a future for Bree. This positive attitude was quoted to a potential patterner by Adrienne Jackson. I learned later that she had said she did not know if what I was doing was going to work, but I was so positive about it and so committed that it was worthwhile giving me a hand.

Walter had changed jobs the second year of programming in the hopes of making more money. He went into the sporting goods business and was on the road three months of the year. During his absence I had friends stay with me. There was always the dread of Bree's having a grand mal seizure and I would not be able to drive the hour-long trip to the hospital in Montreal, holding her at the same time. I felt scared and alone. My knowledge about healing was growing very slowly. The seizures frightened me so much that I would have lived in the hospital waiting room rather than take a chance of being alone. The hospital and its doctors were my security blanket.

Night after night I prayed for guidance… so much so that it was inevitable God and I would become reacquainted. For me, the bottom line was always, "What is best for Bree? Show me what to do and somehow I will manage to get it done."

Despite all it entailed, I was never other than glad that I had ignored all advice and kept Bree at home with me. It boggles my mind that anyone could put their child into an institution… their child, part of them. It seems to me that by doing so they condemn themselves to a lifetime of guilt and to live with that must be hell. The saying goes, "Out of sight, out of mind," but I cannot believe that this is true. I think such a situation would always eat away at you, killing you deep inside, and that somewhere down the road you would have to condemn yourself.

I am so glad I decided to take the less traveled road no matter what lay ahead.

Over the years I have had many people ask me the same question: "What about your life, your free-time, your marriage?" Well, this is my life. My quality of life emotionally, spiritually, physically, and mentally, has been better since Bree's Birth than it was ever before she was born. I love her, learn from her, and care for her. God called me with Bree's birth and I followed even though I had no idea how I would manage or if I could keep it up, yet I had to follow. In eastern countries people consider it an honor to feed monks who come to their doors. Our brain-injured children are our monks, our very special souls and I believe that how we treat them will determine our destiny.

June 11th, 1983:

More from my journal. Almost a year now since we started the program, When I look back over that period, confined to the house, doing program day after endless day, I am always thankful that I waited till I was twenty-seven to get married and that prior to that, I'd spent a couple of summers hitchhiking through Europe. Those memories sustained me and because of them I did not feel I was deprived due to my comparative imprisonment the stimulation program demanded.

I had paid for all my summer traveling in Europe by working and saving the rest of the year. The youngest of six children in a working class family, I was acutely aware of financial matters and had been working at something or other since I was twelve. That was the age I started babysitting and having a paper route. We always had a roof over our heads and there had always been food on the table, but whenever we wanted something beyond the absolute essentials, we had to work to get it. It was not altogether a happy childhood. Sarcasm and criticism seemed to be traits all my family members cultivated. In order to gain respect, one had to become more proficient in it than the others. As well, my father was given to verbal abuse. Fortunately this was balanced out by unconditional love from my mother.

It seems now that the early morning trained I received in my own household was preparing me for what lay ahead with Bree. The sarcasm I had endured during my growing years prepared me for dealing with emotional hurt after she was born… and there was plenty of that! My teenage years as a loner and a reading addict prepared me for the lonely years of work that was to come with Bree. Even that financial problems with suffered were nothing new to me.

June 13th:

Bree and I went to Quebec City with Walter. I had slept poorly the night before and needed to take a day off. Bree and I were both tired and I simply did not have the energy to encourage her to do the program. My restless night had been the result of attending a barbeque with friends and seeing Bree down on the floor, knowing she was desperately wanting to do things the other children were doing so easily. This is one of the hardest things to bear… your child struggling along, crawling or creeping while other children passed her by. There is nothing you can do about it except make sure nobody steps on her, You cannot reveal your agony over the situation, not wanting to make other people feel uncomfortable about something that is not their fault.

June 25th:

We were visited by a family who have an appointment at the Institutes next month for their eight-year-old son who, after six years at a school for the mentally handicapped, is just about able to sit up and feed himself. It soon became obvious that it was the mother who was keen on going and that the father did not want to go. He had all sorts of excuses. It was too expensive, his wife was not strong enough to do such an intensive program, they had another child to be considered, he was on the road a lot for business, and what would happen to their social life? I began to wonder why he had bothered coming to waste our time, but I gave him answers to all the drawbacks he had mentioned and made it clear that if he went to Philadelphia with that attitude, his child would most certainly not be a candidate for a program. That sobered him a little, but my heart went out to the mom as I knew how difficult it must be for her having to cope with someone who had such a negative approach.

June 25th:

Today I learned that the family who had visited were not going to Philadelphia and my first reaction was one of anger on behalf of my child whose parents were not prepared to make any sacrifices for him. They did listen to the objections of the doctors and my second surge of anger was directed at the medical profession. I'd had my fill of doctors who sat in their offices like mini-Gods, telling parents what they should do or not do with their brain-injured children... as casually as if they were discussing a disposable plastic cup! They are not the ones who are ultimately responsible for a child's life.

I feel sorry for mothers who are not confidant enough to listen to their own maternal instincts and stand up to the professionals, asking probing questions and seeking alternatives.

July 13th:

A lackluster day. Nothing special happened and I felt unmotivated, tired and easily irritated. Bree reluctantly crept a minimum amount and only did that after a lot of prodding. I wished she would realize that I was not doing the program for my own fun but in the hopes of making her well enough for us to live like a normal family. Ah well, maybe that would come in the not-too-distant future. In the meantime, all I could do was forced myself to continue... and suppress my annoyance when Walter would take over for a day on the weekend and triumphantly announce how quickly the program was completed, without even noticing how exhausted Bree would be because he rushed her instead of pacing her.

July 20th:

Another eye examination, an easy one this time with no tears from Bree. There was good news… the doctor said that she has come a long way. The right eye seems to be farsighted by fine. The left one, which has a cataract, is a little shortsighted and he wants to try patching it up. He's impressed with her progress and I learn that he has in his files a copy of the newspaper article about her.

August 6th:

For the first time in a year I am somewhere without Bree, spending a day at the Trappist Monastery in Oka, Quebec. All alone… so strange to have all these hours of silence.

August 9th:

We are at Lake George, New York, on our way to Philadelphia for another revaluation. We desperately needed a few days' break, so we stopped off here for a couple of days and I wondered if we'd been wise. Here we are in an over-priced motel with a couple of beers, waiting for Bree to wake up. We owe money and know that if our house doesn't sell soon, our credit cards will be in a terrible state… but once in awhile we try to pretend that we are just like everyone else.

September 17th:

Today we celebrated our sixth wedding anniversary, which actually fell on August 27th, but with the trip to Philadelphia taking place then, this is the first chance we have had to celebrate. I listened to someone on television talking about how lucky the people are who have something definite to do on this earth. Well, at least I know I can survive our problems and be a better person because of it. I have been blessed in that circumstances have forced me to take a look at my life and to decide what has meaning and what I really want to do. I would hate to think that I had gone through life untouched and without growing as a person. Certainly the growth hurts and I sometimes cry and scream over it, but surely that is better than living like a zombie, afraid to feel and popping Prozac.

Growing, to me, is like an eagle who builds a nest on a mountain. Then as it grows and its wings get stronger , it is able to build its nest higher and higher up the mountain and the eagle can then soar with the winds, no matter how fierce they are.

It's funny that I never doubt that Bree will be well. Walter believes that she will be able to walk and talk, but I believe she will become totally well.

September 23rd:

At lunch today I had a gut cry that scared me; a lifetime of pain seeping to the surface. I know that if things do no improve financially, there is no way we can continue the program after January.

October 14th:

I worry about Walter and me. We exist together, but nothing more. We are always tired and overstressed. There is no time for happiness. It it a struggle for survival, taking one step forward and two steps backwards. Deep inside I feel that all things work together for the overall good, but today it is difficult holding that thought. I would like some emotional support. It would be nice to have a hug. Walter doesn't hug.

October 16th:

A big snowstorm has cost us some patterners and I dread to think of the winter ahead. Bree is teething, has developed bronchitis, and is on antibiotics. We missed a chance to sell our house last week. I am still hoping we can sell it and move out by the beginning of December, yet that is looking like a forlorn hope as there is not much time left, even though the house is a give-away at the $50,000 we are asking for it. The real estate market is so bad in Quebec that we are not likely to get more than that. I cannot figure out what God is doing. Surely He does not want us to be left high and dry without patterners all winter.

November 17th:

A phone call came from a mother of a twelve-year-old brain-injured child. She was seeking moral support. Her child is in Montreal during the week and at home on the weekends. I wonder how she felt after our conversation because all I could do was tell her what I was doing. She feels that as we have only one child, I can manage the daily program. She feels she cannot because she has other children. Yet, I know many other families with several children who are coping with the Institutes' program for their brain-injured children. I wonder what makes the difference between two sets of parents... why one will come out fighting and refuse to accept second-best for their child and the other is convinced they are in an unchangeable situation and should just make do?

November 27th:

Marge came by to pattern, shaking her keys as she arrived and left so that Bree will associate her with the sound, just as she knows Hope is the one who arrives with the two little dogs. Marge brought me $60 for Bree. My patterners are such good people. We have been through two weeks of hell with our house being nearly sold, then the deal falling through at the last minute... for some unknown reason.

December 12th:

What a year to look back on! First being taken for a ride over the trust fund that wasn't and then Walter's having to spend January and February in St. John, Quebec, leaving me to cope with the program; being in Philadelphia during their record snowfall. The list goes on with Bree being sick and not having enough money in August for a scheduled revisit. We were so poor that Walter had to sell the colored T.V. he had won as a door prize at a company party. In September we sold our car so that we could continue payments and go to Philadelphia. Thank goodness Walter had a company car. What a hassle it had been coping with more than forty families inspecting the house as potential buyers but not getting a sale. Major household problems were an added concern. The switch on the hot water burned out, the cold water tank wore out, and there were long electricity failures. Bree had several grand mal seizures that lasted at least four hours.

December 16th:

There was an upsetting television program about whether parents have the right to let a brain-injured child die when an operation might have kept him alive. One of my patterners came out strongly on the side of the parents' right to decide if their child should die. I cannot understand that line of thinking.

We had an open invitation to join and after-ski party and, as I finished Bree's program early, we decided to go along. It was obvious from the reaction that they hadn't expected us to come, though they covered it up quickly.

December 26th:

What a Christmas! We have been having a difficult time with Bree the past few weeks and her results for her next evaluation are not going to be good. There seems to be nothing I can do about it. Neurologically she is falling behind her peers; the older she gets, the wider the cap. We need a massive breakthrough. Why is it taking Bree so long to talk? Sometimes I am so wiped out and feel impatient, sad, and hopeless, but that does not get me anywhere. Can I ever catch up? Maybe I am burned out like people warned. I am basically doing this alone.

Chapter 11

January 25th, 1984:

This is the start of a new year. The house was sold January 19th, four days after we returned from Philadelphia. The Institutes has set walking and talking as Bree's goal for her next visit there, so there is a lot of work ahead for Bre and me. Walter will be away a lot as he has two sporting goods shows to attend. Last weekend I had a young student from Western Canada staying with us. I get her services free under a Government scheme that pays her. She is a television addict and watches from the time she gets up in the morning till she goes to bed at night, doing whatever jobs that can be done in front of the screen.

February 7th:

Nothing frustrates me as much as Bree going blank on me. Sometimes she is full of energy and talkative and the next day totally unresponsive. It drives me nuts.

February 8th:

Pat Carignan from the Mentally Handicapped Center called to ask how Bree was doing, She wants to arrange for some parents to come and see what we are doing. She thinks knowing of the program may be useful for them. The responsibility scares me in a way because I feel I have a lot of work still in front of me and a lot to learn.

February 16th:

I have a cold and feel miserable. Bree has a cold and an ear infection and she is on antibiotics. I asked Walter to stay home from work and look after Bree, so I could just stay in bed, but he refused, saying he had work to do. I would never ask him to miss work unless I felt at the end of my rope. I need his support, but he is not coming through for me. I feel angry and alone. His job is not even bringing in enough money to pay for the program and he seems to have lost interest and does all he can to get out of doing any of the program with her. I don't appreciate his attitude.

March 8th:

Bree had a grand mal attack last Friday and we spent a day and a half at the hospital. Every night since we came home, she has awakened crying. After seven nights of being awakened and stressed, I feel worn out.

June 6th:

We are into the first month of a two-month break that the Institutes gives families after they have done the stimulation program for two complete years. For the first five days of freedom, I developed a headache, trying to adjust to having nothing to do. Walter was away, so I stayed with my parents. Mom let me sleep in every morning… heavenly! Walter came home from his business trip and stayed for four days (in a bitchy mood) and then left for three days of meeting in Montreal. His growing indifference to the program has culminated in a statement that he wants the program to be only five days a week instead of seven. His attitude is that the program is great as long as someone else is doing the work. He hasn't been doing any of it lately. These days he has absolutely no patience with Bree. She realizes it and will not settle down with him, so once again I have to do everything for her. We took the opportunity to go Nashville where Walter was to attend a sporting goods show. The trip was an expense-paid one it gave us a badly needed chance to talk.

August 20th:

Days today test my faith. I have had diarrhea since Thursday and am impatient with Bree. I feel as though I cam holding on by a shoestring.

August 30th:

I am celebrating my birthday alone at Gibby's Restaurant. Walter has forgotten it… again - and I refuse to remind him. It's the continuing story of his taking my giving and I wonder how good our marriage really is. His desire to be free gets me. He wants to have good times and no responsibilities. He does not understand how superficial that life is. We have found a nice house to rent in the village of St. Sauveur and life is much better for me. It feels comfortable to be within reach of people and to be able to put Bree in her stroller and take her to the Post Office and the grocery store.

I rented our spare room to a daughter of one of my patterners who is moving out of the area. The daughter wants to finish her last year of high school here in the Laurentians. She stayed with us for five months, an interesting experience. She was a good kid but accustomed to a lively environment, quite different from our very structured one.

After we returned from Nashville, Bree seemed to be getting constant colds and eventually developed pneumonia. The Institutes took her off the floor exercises for a month to give her a chance to build up her strength. Physically she was getting weaker. Although she had been taking vitamins for over two years, she was still susceptible to any infection that prevented her from doing a full program. One worry that sat at the back of my mind was the fact that the doctors had predicted a five-year life span at the most. She was nearly that now and getting weaker. I felt I was in a race against time.

December 18th:

We have just returned from what was to be our last trip to the Institutes. There was no money for further trips and, much as I hated to admit it, I could not carry out the program without emotional support. I was not getting any. During our stay in Philadelphia one of the families from Texas told me about someone in their area who was doing the program but had just put their child on a diet called Macrobiotics. The mother thought this might be important to me because that little girl had seizures and was very much like Bree. My interest was aroused. I would consider anything that might lessen the need to cope with seizures. Next to the thought of Bree dying, they were what I feared most.

An hour from home, Bree started throwing up due to an infected throat and she was put on antibiotics. Walter is not happy and is thinking of leaving us. I have told him to make his own decision about that but said that he will have to figure out someway to support us as I have no intention of cutting back on Bree's needs. By investigating some other avenues for dealing with her problems, I learned that there is an osteopathic doctor right here. Also, I have received information about macrobiotic cooking. I am still hesitant about anything new and pray that God will guide and protect us.

Walter is National Sales Manager for his company and travels a great deal and is away many weekends. When he does have time off, he spends it skiing, windsurfing, climbing, or running. We are dealing with Bree's situation very differently. I was reading and studying anything I could find and my life and outlook were changing constantly. If I heard of anything new, I felt I must look into it to see if there was something of value for Bree. Whatever I decide doesn't bother Walter as long as he isn't expected to do anything about it. He spends his evening watching television and drinking beer. He has stopped giving Bree her twice-weekly baths which he used to do while I prepared supper. He pays very little attention to her these days.

Bree was constantly having small seizures which made her fall down and she was constantly constipated. I had to use suppositories daily and that bothered me. It seemed to me that it made sense to look into Bree's diet even though the people at the Institutes and our doctor thought her diet was an excellent one. She had been breast-fed for eleven months and then I added a formula for six months, thinking she needed extra nutrients. I prepared all her food myself, making a quantity and freezing some, so that it would be handy any time. Many people thought I was giving myself a lot of extra work instead of using commercial baby foods.

Bree is now four and a half years old and we are about to take a major step. She has done very well on the stimulation program. At the beginning she was so little and her only movement was to roll over. She did not focus on anything and had no tactile response to touch. Her advancement is gratifying. The only change I could see that could possibly improve her health was her diet. Vitamins had not kept her from having frequent colds that required antibiotic and she was still having lots of seizure activity.

I began reading books on nutrition, seeking answers. The previous spring one of the Institutes' Directors, Mary Kett, had given a lecture on using grains and beans. She had recommended two books that I bought but had not read. I got these out along with my notes on her lecture plus some recipes that had been handed out. I also bought some books on vegetarian cooking for children.

All that fall I tried making changes in Bree's menu, experiment with her food, looking for results. One of the first things I did was take her off dairy food entirely because I had learned that some brain-injured children were allergic to these foods. I wondered if there was a connection between them and Bree's seizures. I had never given Bree sugar. To me, it fell into the category of "junk foods". That fall I read William Dufty's *Sugar Blues*. His book showed me I had been right.

Once, when I had been staying with the hospital with Bree, there was a brain-injured teenager in her room. His worried and concerned mother was hovering over him. She told me he had a seizure while eating and, as she was telling me this, she was feeding him chocolates and a soft drink… the exact food, I felt, would be likely to trigger a seizure. It was not my place to tell her so, but it was hard to watch. It was interesting to note that none of the hospital staff saw that what she was doing was undesirable in any way.

I heard that Mary Kett had gone to Boston to study Macrobiotics and that sounded interesting. She had been a Director at the Institutes for fifteen years and, knowing how involved and dedicated all the staff were, I felt that if she had gone to study Macrobiotics more closely there must be something in it.

I hated telling the Institutes we could not afford to return, but fortunately they understood our problem (It took us four years to pay our debt to them, but they patiently accepted this). Certainly I could continue doing a home program, yet I knew this would not work as well without the goals and the revisits to look forward to. Also, I would miss seeing the other families and sharing our experiences. We were like wartime buddies, the war being our fight against brain injury and the ignorance people had about it.

On our last visit, Walter was very difficult about one of the program selections we were being taught. I wanted him to stop questioning it, as I would be the one doing it anyway. He did not want to be involved in the program anymore. I was getting tired of his constant complaining about it and the money we were spending.

The only thing that might make it easier for me to cut back on the intensity of the program, and I felt it inevitably would, was the fact that Bree was weaker and we did not seem to be getting anywhere in any case. The seizures had gotten in the way of things and I felt that now it was better to concentrate on improving her general health. Then, once she was stronger, we could start back on the program. At least I knew now that it was available.

It would be a relief to have Walter off my back, to restore peace in the household, and the health issues would keep me focused. Everything else has to be secondary to improving Bree's general condition.

Chapter 12

The first day we got back from Philadelphia, I made phone calls that got me the information I needed about the macrobiotic diet. I called the Kushi Institute in Boston for a local contact. They referred me to Mike Burns, a naturopath who had moved back to Montreal the previous month. I saw him on the twenty-first of December and it was an interesting experience. He was very caring, not like other naturopaths I had met. I was impressed by his excellent interaction with his own children. He gave me an outline of what Bree should eat and told me where to find a store that stocked the foods needed for this diet.

There were no more little frozen cubes of food in the refrigerator for Bree. Everything was cooked daily and her diet included whole grains, fresh vegetable, dried beans, seeds, nuts, sea vegetables, and some fermented items that were new to me: miso, tempeh, and tofu. I spent a lot of time reading about Macrobiotics and cooking what was required.

The first sign of change was the curing of Bree's chronic constipation, which pleased me enormously.

Walter was not at all pleased with the new regime. He didn't mind if Bree and I followed this "newfangled" diet but he had been brought up on one consisting of meat potatoes, cheese, eggs, peanut butter, and a great deal of ice cream and cookies. He wasn't about to change. It was easier for me because I was used to having porridge, homemade soup, fish, beans, milk, and vegetables. My family's main meat meal was on Sunday nights. I had the feeling that we were reverting to an old-style way of eating. Grain and beans along with local vegetables used to be the foundation of diets, at least on the farms.

Walter:

So Wendy and Bree were going Macrobiotic.

The general sense of this diet made sense to me, but I must confess there were parts of the teaching that didn't make sense. I did not understand how pots and pans that had been used to cook meats could not be used for vegetables, but Wendy insisted they couldn't. I found it difficult to understand why a gas stove was a necessary item... that electric energy was unhealthy.

I was not a full convert to that diet. I was still eating meat and dairy products and found it hard to adhere to the rules of the new diet. I didn't want to stop Wendy and Bree from following the rules, but it sure caused some arguments in our kitchen. I ended up cooking my own meals with my own pots and pans... and ordering lots of pizza.

One reason I was slow to the diet was that I was spending a great deal of time traveling and eating in restaurants. Also, I had grown up in a meat-eating family and loved the taste of heavy, rich food. The meals Wendy was cooking were not spicy, never fried, and not tasty to my jaded palate.

Despite my resistance to the new diet, Bree was doing well on it. She ate with no problems and her chronic constipation had suddenly vanished. For years Wendy had been giving her what was considered the best possible food, but nothing made any significant change till Wendy tried the macrobiotic diet. This new way of life, new philosophy, and new foods were to prove a great discovery for our family, however I was extremely stubborn about accepting it.

Wendy:

A could of weeks into the change of diet, I thought I should inform the pediatrician at the Institute about what I was doing. Her main concern was to ensure that Bree was getting enough calories. Bree is thin enough and has always been slow to put on weight. I tried to check out the calorie total but couldn't get an adequate answer, so I phoned the Kushi Institute. The woman who answered the phone, Suzanne Jenson, hadn't had much experience with brain-injured children but offered to put me in touch with someone who had experience. That someone turned out to be Mary Kett from Philadelphia, whose house in Boston Suzanne was sharing.

Again, it turned out to be perfect timing for Suzanne was doing the phone answering for a two-hour period to help out a friend. She had never done it before. It was as if she was placed there to make the connection!

When I had told Mary what I had learned from the Macrobiotic books, she made an exciting proposal. She said it is essential to learn about the cooking process first-hand and offered to give me lessons if I could get to Boston and added I could stay with her. The only cost would be getting there. She also suggested that I bring along a sitter for Bree, so I could give one hundred percent of my attention to the lessons. I was excited about her offer and started looking for ways to take her up on it. One problem was that the only time I could use Walter's company car was when he flew out of town on business.

Things moved faster than I had expected or even hoped. The following day in a casual conversation in health food store, I was told about the possibility of getting a student who was studying nutrition at the University of Montreal to come along as the sitter. That night Walter came home to announce that, in two week's time, he would be going out of town for a week.

We left for Boston in a blinding snowstorm and could barely see fifty feet in front of us until we reached the U.S. border. We missed out exit in Boston and found Mary's place by grace as I had never driven in Boston before. I was concerned about what it would be like living with someone else for a week, especially so because I wasn't sure about Mary's lifestyle and diet. Macrobiotics and the Buddhist religion sometimes go hand-in-hand. The next morning Mary took me by surprise when she said,

"We won't start cooking until ten o'clock because I go to Mass first." My fears melted away. I don't know what I kept questioning God. I should have known by then that as long as I was acting in goodwill, I would not be steered in the wrong direction.

It is easy to accept the position that food has a strong influence on the quality of life. In Macrobiotics one eats to achieve a balance of foods... whole cereal grains and organic vegetables form a major part of the diet, along with soy products, sea vegetables, soups, and beans (which I had already been experimenting with). In reading about this subject, so new to me, I learned that we change our body cells every seven years and our brain cells every twelve years. The latter was probably the most important fact of all because of Bree's problem and it gave me hope.

In almost five years, I had made no progress, in eliminating seizures, with doctors, hospitals, and medications. Bree had to have stronger medicines as time went on. I was worried about their side effects, especially after I learned that it was not usual for pharmaceutical companies to list pages of possible side effects with all drugs... side effects we the public never knew about.

A major ambition of mine was to have Bree medication-free and seizure-free. Maybe with Macrobiotics I could achieve that goal. To my mind, medication was not the answer to a seizure problem, especially not a long term one. If one is healthy, one does not experience seizures. There has to be an imbalance somewhere that causes the body to react that when when there is too much stress for the body to defuse.

Mary Kett was the perfect teacher for someone in my situation. She had seen hundreds of brain-injured children in her years in Philadelphia. I had four intensive days under her guidance and it was fantastic. The techniques she taught me were not simply cooking, for she turned them into an art form. I was no longer eating because I was hungry. Now everything I ate and fed Bree was something to strengthen my body, to help regenerate itself.

I returned home after several days, charged with new energy and motivation and with a much better idea of what Macrobiotics was all about. This was not just a diet, it was a way of life. I really liked it. It felt truly spiritual. I made plans as I drove home. We had only a small kitchen, so the first thing I would have to do was organize it for efficiency. Until I could persuade Walter to buy a gas stove, I would have to get a camping stove.

My first act was to post Bree's weekly menu on the refrigerator door. I had every intention of following the diet to the letter because I was afraid that if I didn't get it right Bree would not get better. At first I was spending up to four hours a day cooking, but gradually macrobiotic cooking became a part of my life. I could spend less time cooking and still get excellent results. In those early days I was quite tense about it. I would do anything to get rid of Bree's seizures.

I tried to ignore Walter's obvious resentment of the time I was spending over the stove. This was for Bree and I was getting good results. I had her off all medication within a year and that alone was worth the effort. Her need for antibiotics for frequent colds was lessening markedly and I was much healthier, too. I appreciated the changes Bree was going through and my health was also improving by eating along with her.

Five months into the program, I returned to Boston for an appointment with Michio Kushi that Mary had arranged. I wanted Walter to go with us and though he refused at first, he changed his mind later that week before we were due to leave. He decided to go with us for a few day only for he had an appointment in Chicago and would fly there from Boston, leaving the car with us.

Mary's house was under construction and, as a result of that, I saw how different atmospheres affect the result of a day's cooking. The first night the food we had cooked was delicious, yet the second the food was much better, We wondered about that. We had cooked in the same way, so why the difference? There was something happening on the first day that was absent on the second one. A carpenter had been hammering outside the kitchen most of the first day.

Now anyone who has no knowledge of macrobiotic philosophy might find it difficult to understand that the hammering would have any effect at all on what we were doing. Yet, according to the macrobiotic philosophy, it is believed that the energy of the food is important and that the health of mind and body of the cook has an effect on the healing energy of the food. There is a big difference between an angry cook and one who is at peace with his or her life and surroundings.

Another influence is believed to be the way the food is cooked. I had noticed that the rice I cooked at my parents' house never tasted as good as what I cooked at home even though I used the same rice, even using my own pressure cooker. The only difference was that they had an electric stove and we were cooking with gas.

In the spring of 1985, Walter started talking about moving closer to Montreal. I liked living in the village of St. Sauveur, but it didn't really matter where we lived as long as I could get the foods I needed for Bree and I was already doing a lot of my food shopping in Montreal. We were to move in July and in May, Annette arrived at our house in a very poor state of health. She had helped me enormously during the stimulation program and there was no question about her staying with us until she was better. After two months of macrobiotic cooking, she was ready to go out on her own. I was kept busy with Bree, cooking, and packing to be ready for the move.

Our new house was in Pierrefonds, a suburb of Montreal only ten minutes from Walter's office. I didn't figure we'd stay there very long, but that it would do for the time being. Walter's parents lived an hour north and mine and hour south, so we could escape the city on weekends. A couple of months after moving in, we went to Gaspe for a vacation at my parents' place. Walter was happy windsurfing and I always enjoyed going back to the place where I was born. I felt very safe at the cabin that my grandfather Gilker had left my family. It had been made from a railroad boxcar and had a direct view of the bay. It contained all we needed – two bedrooms, a small kitchen with a gas stove, and a living room, but no phone or television.

Mary Kett came to spend time with us that summer, along with Lee Pattison one of the first people we had met at the Institute. We foraged for sea vegetables in Chaleur Bay and found great crops of Irish Moss and Dulse. When we spread it out on the lawn, my relatives thought we were nuts. Why would anyone want to eat seaweed? The sea garden is much like a land garden in that you have to know what is a sea vegetable and what is an overgrown weed. You also have to know the correct harvesting time.

Mary and Lee went sightseeing and collected fossils and we'd all gather for supper each evening. Lee stayed at a local bed-and-breakfast in a historical house a short distance away. She is a writer and born story-teller, which added a great deal of fun and entertainment to our meals together. Both Lee and Mary are seasoned travelers and fit in well wherever they are, so it was not like having company that had to be entertained. It was great to have two people who had worked with brain-injured children, who understood what was happening in our household. For a short time I felt truly supported.

That summer Mary expanded my horizons. She recommended a course called "Silva Mind Control" and introduced me to two books that were to give my spiritual life a boost – In Tune With The Infinite by Ralph Waldo Trine and The Door Of Everything by Ruby Nelson. They both dealt with positive thinking and spoke of drawing to yourself what you wanted most and what you feared most, so that instead of thinking of Bree dying and that, I could visualize her becoming totally well and happy. The books turned a light on within me where there had been total darkness. They game me a lot to think about.

I knew for a fact that I was overprotective of Bree, fearing I would lose her. She was not yet at the point with her health that I could pull back much in my care giving, but I could change my mental attitude and and this way, my outward attitude would change. I knew I had been guilty of thoughtlessly making comments about how long and skinny she was, thinking this was okay, when a positive comment would be to say how tall and strong she as. I was still working my way through healing all the sarcastic, supposedly loving comments from my own childhood. Up to this point in time, I had worked hard at maintaining Bree at as high a peak of physical health I could manage. Now we were to start on another level it and would add to our daily routine of working with food for the mind as well as for the body, on the premise that, as well as being what we eat, we are also what we think. Food for the body may be the more important element, yet the food we eat sends nutrients to the brain and the brain is the command center of our bodies.

I remembered a horrible experience I had read about that took place in the concentration camps in World War II. Prisoners were told to put their hands through a hole in the wall and were then told their hands would be cut off and they would be left to bleed to death. They could not see their hands but they could feel something sharp against their skin and then could hear what sounded like blood dripping on to the floor. It was water, but they had no way of knowing that. They believed what they were told and they died... killed by belief.

After returning from Gaspe, I had a chance to watch all the Kushi lectures on video tapes that had been loaned to me and I learned a great deal. I also checked on the Silva program and signed up for a November course being given in Montreal. I saw this program as another healing tool for Bree. I had always thought that I was a positive thinking, yet it was obvious I still had a long way to go. I got more out of the course than Walter. He was bored and kept nodding off during the lectures.

Chapter 13

The following fall and winter I began helping two other Montreal families who had brain-injured children, seeing this as an opportunity to return some of the help that had been offered to me. I felt that the healing information I had was too good not to be spread as widely as possible. There were other parents, I felt sure, who were in the position I had been in years earlier, needing this sort of holistic information – but not knowing where to find it.

One problem I had was in pacing myself. I was so excited about sharing this information with others that I tried too quickly to pass on what had taken me years to learn. I tended to try to do things too much for other mothers and had to learn to pull back to prevent exhausting myself. When I first started teaching macrobiotic cooking to those interesting, I was giving two hundred percent to people who were barely able to grasp fifty percent and found myself becoming wiped out after a succession of classes.

There were some who did not want to do any work themselves and this was difficult and disappointing. They were looking for someone else to provide the answers to their problems . They were looking for someone else to provide the answers to their problems. They wanted the results I got without having to give up anything or change their lives in any way. People who were willing to stick around with holistic healing and a macrobiotic diet didn't need everything done for them. What they needed was a helping hand and to be guided to the right books, courses, and people.

There is a saying by an Elder of the Cree Indians that states: "Before healing can take place, the poison must be exposed." I have found that many of the parents of brain-injured children have years of subconscious guilt poisoning them within which has to be dealt with.

Learning that I had to heal myself first before I could heal Bree was an eye-opener for me. I had to expose the poisons of blaming God, blaming myself, and mourning the child I never had. Recognizing Bree as a gift and not as a punishment for something I had done was a major step forward for me. Then the healing began... and endless, wondrous journey.

The first Christmas after we moved to Montreal was one of the worst I had experienced. My parents lived in an old English style house and they asked us to join them for Christmas. My brother's two children lived about five hundred feet away and they came to spend the night. The following morning everyone was so excited about opening presents. I asked if they minded waiting just twenty minutes until I gave Bree her breakfast because experience taught me that she would get petit mal seizures if I didn't maintain a regular eating schedule. My father responded quickly, saying in a very rude way that they would not wait and went into the living room.

I was stunned and hurt. On that Christmas morning he had written Bree off as a grandchild who did not matter. Everything centered around the other two grandchildren and Bree was just there. I fed Bree and then Walter and I decided to go for a drive. I could not be around such rudeness, such thoughtlessness. Driving around the countryside, I found myself crying and crying. How could my own family not see that our daughter was beautiful and not include her

One of the most upsetting aspects was that nobody seemed to feel that anything was wrong in excluding her. They acted on our return as if nothing had happened. I suppose I should have been immune to such incidents of rudeness. After all, when my oldest brother came into the house or when we met at his restaurant, family members would greet one another, children included, but always ignored Bree. Because she could not respond physically, as the other children could, it was as though she could not <u>feel</u> anything either. It scares me when I see people writing brain-injured children off. How can some children receive love because they are "normal" while other cannot because they are hurt?

The following spring Walter was laid off and it looked as if his company was to be sold. He was kept on salary for four months, provided with the services of a job-finding agency, and given the use of the company car for a few months.

We were prepared to leave Pierrefonds but before we did, Bree had two grand mal seizures. We took her to the hospital, but the experience was so devastating that we never took her there again. Bree had been napping and Walter was off wind-surfing. I was still watching Bree carefully because I had mapped out a pattern of her seizure activity and noted certain times of the year she was more prone to have them. These times were on the longest day of the year, the shortest day, when there was a full moon or change of seasons, and around the first of March. Also, she always had them when she was sleeping. One these "danger days," I avoided stressful activities and increased my watchfulness.

During her nap I checked and found that she was breathing strangely. I became alarmed when I worked on her and she did not respond, so I called an ambulance, leaving a message for Walter with the neighbors. The doctor who came in the ambulance didn't want me to ride with Bree and would not listen when I told him not to give her a normal drug dose as it would be too strong for her. I had to sit up front with the driver. At Montreal Children's Hospital they rushed Bree into the emergency room but would not let me go with her. This had never happened to me before and I felt alone and scared. I told the nurses that my husband had always stayed with her and that as long as he was not there, I wanted to be with Bree. They would not listen to me, saying they were following normal procedure.

I began to wonder if Bree had died on the way to the hospital because no one would give me a straight answer. Riding in the ambulance, I had heard the doctor talking in French to the driver, telling him to hurry as Bree's breathing labored. Finally, two doctors came to talk with me. The nurses must have to them that I thought they weren't being honest with me. They explained that they were very concerned and wanted to put Bree on a respirator. I did not know what to do except try to phone Mary in Boston, so I said I had to call my doctor in Boston before making any decisions. I called Mary's house and Suzanne was the only one there. She said I would have to go along with the doctor's recommendation. While I was making the phone call, Bree had stabilized and though she was to be sent to intensive care, she no longer needed to be put on the respirator.

I went with Bree to the intensive care room and then called a girl friend to come and lend me support until Walter arrived. He showed up about two hours later. Walter stayed with Bree and my friend drove me home, so I could get some clothes and food I would need for Bree. I was just going through the motions trying to get back to the hospital as soon as possible. I settled in with Bree and Walter went back home. This was one of my least favorite places to be. Intensive care units which are filled with the beeping of monitor alarms, the humming of motorized beds, and the pumping of ventilators rank alongside of airplane passenger cabins and factory floors as primary hazards to health and hearing. There was no way I would leave her there alone. I had had enough hospital experiences to stick right next to Bree.

The nurses and doctors in extensive car and I did not see eye to eye on a few things. I knew Bree's seizure pattern well and it was obvious to be that she was out of the initial activity and need to sleep off the effects of the drugs she had been given. I could could actually take her home, I felt, but the hospital had its rules about patients admitted for overnight stays and I finally agreed to it, letting them know that I planned to take her home in the morning immediately after the doctor's rounds. In the meantime the intravenous needle in her arm was making Bree restless. I ashed to have it removed, but hospital rules said that it had to stay until the doctor's next visit. Rules, not comfort, mattered. I did win a minor victory about taking "vital signs." Checking every hour was disturbing Bree at a time when sleep was needed the most. I said that as I was sleeping literally with her in my arms, I could be relied on to notice any change, however minor.

The nurse was not happy about having a parent decide what was best for her own child, but over the years I had developed enough confidence to insist on doing what I thought was right for Bree. The staff expected me to stay in the waiting room, but I refused to Bree's side. At first I tried to sleep in a chair beside her bed. The bed was adult sized and during the night, I climbed in beside Bree. It was more comfortable than sleeping in a chair. Once during the night I caught the nurse trying to take the vital signs. Incredible… wake someone up who is sleeping soundly to make sure she is okay.

We were ready to go home the next morning, but no doctor had come to see her. I was told I needed him to check her out. A nurse pointed out the doctor. He was walking down the corridor. It was the first time I had seen him. When I caught up with him, he was leaving. It was obvious from his reaction when I introduced himself that he had been told about this "difficult" mother.

When I told him I was taking Bree home, his response was,

"You're wrong." This was a bit too much for me to accept from a man who had never met me or talked with me, so I replied,

"No, I am not wrong." He turned around and walked down the corridor saying,

"You are wrong." This was our entire conversation. I immediately called Walter and asked him to join me as soon as possible, figuring I needed some back-up to get Bree home safe and sound. All because I was not willing to follow procedures blindly! Yes, I questioned everything. After all, doctors are human beings, not gods, and they are fallible.

I remember once when Bree's chart had been left with is to take to the next doctor, Walter opened it up to see what had been said about her. He found a comment that I was "far too emotional about her child." Interesting… in Bernie Siegel's book, *Love, Medicine, and Miracles*, he points out that the patients who survive life threatening situations are the "difficult ones." The patients with the lowest survival rates are the ones who accept everything without question. I am positive that Bree is alive today because I left traditional medicine behind when it did not serve her needs anymore.

Siegel also write in another book, Prescriptions For Living, that a doctor is in a position to learn a great deal about being human, but to learn from people he is working with, a physician must first learn to ignore the noninvolvement credo taught in medical schools. He or she must begin to view patients as people rather than cases… to love them even and to let them know that a doctor needs love, too.

Walter arrived and then the doctor dame with five student doctors in tow. We were asked to leave while they examined Bree. We said we were not leaving, that they could examine her while we were present. They all left in a huff. One nurse who was sympathetic towards us hurried after them. We don't know what happened, but the head doctor came back alone five minutes later to do the check-up. He said he would prescribe anticonvulsant drugs for Bree, but when we asked him if they would make her seizure-free, he said he could not guarantee that they would. We pointed out that she had been having fewer seizures since discontinuing her medication and there seemed no point in giving them to her. As that was our attitude, he insisted that we sign a form that we stated we were disregarding his recommendations, which we agreed to do quite willingly.

It was interesting to note that, prior to this episode, the doctor had been insisting Bree be examined by him and his students and that we could not be there. Now, not only was it not necessary to examine her, but he had just wanted us out of there. This hospital had many doctors in training and Bree with her rare syndrome made an interesting study. We didn't want our daughter to be poked at as an interesting study!

We were more than happy to take Bree home. The seizures were pasat. She was a little sleepy from the drugs, but how lovely it was to wrap her up and take her home.

I called Mary to let her know that we were home after that frightening experience and we had an interesting conversation. She proposed that I was now in a position to decide whether to keep Bre home when she had a seizure or take her to a hospital. Bree's system was getting "cleaner" from being on the macrobiotic diet and it was becoming almost more dangerous to go to a hospital because it was difficult to get a doctor to understand our way of life, to see how being on the macrobiotic system made it so her body needed less medication than what is considered normal levels.

I was dubious about not taking her to the hospital because I had been told for years that Bree might die if I did not get her there as soon as possible when she had a seizure. Mary had me look at this idea from a different angle.

"Think of the worst that could happen. If the worst did happen, how would you want it to be?" That started me crying instantly. The worst was that Bree could die. If she did, I would rather have her die in my arms at home than with stranger in the emergency room of a hospital where I was not allowed to be with her. I could not imagine how abandoned she would feel.

Well, I thought, *maybe she has had her last grand mal attack and I won't be faced with that decision.* At that moment, I felt I could not deal with it.

Our lease in Pierrefonds expired at the end of June, 1986 and since Walter didn't have a job, we were reluctant to rent another house, so we arranged to move into my parents' home, hopefully for only the months of July. My mother was agreeable, but my father was not supportive. My parents would be at the Gaspe cabin for three weeks in July, so we would not be together for too long; plus, their three-bedroom house was large enough for us not to be underfoot. We moved our belongings into their garage. I set up my little camping gas stove on top of a small wood stove in the kitchen that was not used in the summer. In this way my cooking for Bree would not interfere with my father's cooking.

It was not an easy or comfortable period. My mother preferred my macrobiotic food and this annoyed my father. He resorted to all sorts of petty actions to make things difficult. the problem was that with my arrival, he saw some of the control he had always exercised over my mother vanishing. She didn't like to cook and he had some control of the household by doing all the cooking.

Fortunately, they were away when Bree had her next attack of grand mal, because he decided to handle it without going to a hospital. Walter began masking and I put cold compresses on her forehead and the nape of her neck. I called Mary Kett for advice and moral support. It was five o'clock in the morning, but she did not mind. I think she put in some good prayer work for me that morning. I knew were were doing the right thing but I was scared to death. This was going against everything the doctors had told us, including the dread that further brain damage might be caused by an unchecked seizure.

Two hours later Bree came out of it, took a deep breath, and fell into and exhausted sleep. Walter looked at me and marveled at how calm I had been during the whole episode. That struck me as odd because calm was far from how I had been feeling. I was just doing what needed to be done to save my little one, as I begged and prayed. The rest of the summer passed uneventfully except for a few small seizures that were eased by cold compresses.

My sister and her family from British Columbia (4000 miles away) visited, her first in several years. The house was large enough to hold everyone and we came up with the idea of celebrating Christmas in August. It was a chance to have all the family together.

Walter had the offer of two jobs, one in Montreal and the other in Toronto. The Toronto one looked to be the better and it paid some $10,000 a year more. He flew there to check it out. Walter was astonished to find out how expensive rentals were, much more expensive than in Montreal, yet people were lined up to get them. We were lucky to get a three-bedroom house, but it was twice as much rent as we had paid in Montreal. I was worried about how we would make ends meet. Bree and I had driven to Toronto with Walter on the weekend we found this house. We grabbed it because of the lack of time and choice. While we were driving back to our hotel, I heard on the radio and announcement that students at York University were looking for rooms to rent and I looked to my left, seeing a sign that said, "York University," which was less than a mile from where we had just signed a lease. I asked Walter if he heard the ad. He said he hadn't.

I said, "We just need to put our name on the list of rooms to let." This was a case of what Carl Jung called "Synchronicity," a run of coincidences connected so meaningfully that their chance concurrence would represent an astronomical degree of improbability.

We had a month in which to make the move, to say goodbye to friends, hire a moving van, and head west for a new way of life. Walter drive the moving van and I followed in the car with Bree and Sam. Nothing had been said about pets and we didn't dare bring up the subject. Our one-hundred-pound labrador was a member of our family and we took a chance that pets were allowed.

I asked the University of York to list us for a male non-smoking student and within weeks there were three possibilities. The first was not prepared to pay the going rate of rent, the second was obviously a night owl and party animal, and the third was Horace, a young man from Trinidad who moved in while Walter was away on a business trip in Vancouver, I felt a little uneasy about that. However Horace proved to be a very quiet person who needed the stability of a family. We saw very little of him as he went to school, went out occasionally with friends, and the rest of the time he studied and slept. I never saw anyone who slept as much as Horace did!

Our house was in north central Toronto and we lived there thirteen months. The job has seemed to be the answer to our financial problems and the city was clean and organized, but we felt confined. The city was in the midst of a building boom and there was a brick shortage because so many houses were being erected... all six feet from each other.

I found it very difficult living in the city, having been raised in the semi-country. It was even harder coping with the endless traffic. Toronto was not the financial answer we had expected it to be, Certainly Walter's salary was high, but so were rents, food, and everything else. I spent a great deal of time on the phone seeking services for Bree, but the agencies were so overworked with the influx of new arrivals that a waiting list of a year was not unusual. I was interested in finding a tutor to come to the house to teach Bree. When I telephoned the school district, they were interested in finding out why she was not attending school and sent someone to check it out. They had nothing they could offer us and the interviewer, at the time of her visit, said that teachers could learn from me as I was obviously doing more on my own than any school she knew of could do.

Bree was due for an appointment at the Kushi Institute in Boston that October and Mary arranged for us to stay with a macrobiotic family the second weeks of our stay to experience how a large family maintained this lifestyle. I learned a great deal about this from Diane Avoli and her seven daughters. What impressed me the most was how quiet and sane the household was with seven children.

Apart from our Boston visit, life was very routine, busier than ever as I had decided to make all of Bree's clothes. At this point in time all her bedding was cotton and she was sleeping on a cotton futon. I wanted one hundred percent cotton clothing for her and that was becoming increasingly difficult to buy.

That winter I found a New Age bookstore and became acquainted with Louise Hays' Heal Your Life and Shakti Gawain's Creative Visualization. I loved the idea proposed by these books that we are responsible for creating our own reality. This meant I had a choice and could change my reality with some work. I also read Steven Halpern's Sound Health that was about how sounds can affect our health as our bodies resonate automatically to them. While I was working with Bree during the day, I played Halpern and Hay cassettes as background.

There was a sadness for us that winter. We had been noticing our faithful Sam was slowing down on his runs but attributed it to increasing age. However, on what was a routine checkup by the vet, we learned there was something seriously wrong with his heart. This was a particular blow to Walter for Sam had been his close companion for almost ten years. Sam had been a comfort to me during many lonely nights when I was trying to figure out what to do to help Bree and he had always been there to protect Bree and me while Walter was on the road. At the Guelph

University Veterinary College we were told that we should put him to sleep as his heart condition was a serious one that often affected large dogs, coming on suddenly. We couldn't make such a decision then, so we took him with us, along with some pills to reduce the accumulation of water in his lungs.

Thinking about deliberately ending his life seemed unbearable and we postponed the decision and instead put him on our macrobiotic diet. We decided we would give him all the good food and extra live that we could and we hoped to keep him alive at least until our next trip to the Gaspe, so we would be able to have a last vacation together.

I was talking with my mom one day and she mentioned that she had been reading an "East/West" magazine I had left behind and she wondered if I had read an article about crystals. I told her I had noticed the article but that was all and asked how it could be of any help to me. Mom urged me to read this article that was about a man named Marcel Vogel who was doing research with crystals in California. A senior scientist for twenty-seven years, he had designed the magnetic disc coating used in computers and held over a hundred patents for various inventions. Now he was working on the capacity of quartz crystals to heal. This is where I found myself taking a sudden interest. Was Mom once again my guidepost?

I didn't understand the connection between crystals and healing. Science had been my weakest subject in school and even when Dr. Vogel's secretary put me in touch with people in Ontario, I floundered because I didn't have the basic knowledge I needed to comprehend what they were trying to explain to me.

I called California thinking that contact with the source might be the way to go. Another synchronistic "coincidence" had me talking to Dr. Vogel himself. His secretary was away from her desk and he picked up the phone as he passed it. He listened to what I had to say about Bree, her condition, and our financial status, which precluded a visit to San Jose where he was working at the time. When I had finished, he said that I was to call him, no charge, on Wednesday morning at nine. California time, after he returned from Mass. He said that it was Lent and that he had given up sugar and that he would work with us over the phone. He became my spiritual guide and a true healthy father figure. IT was an interesting period. He told me when he used his thirteen-sided crystal to do long distance healing by phone, the crystal got so hot at times that he could hardly hold it. He seemed to tune into Bree's thoughts and feelings and then relayed them to me. He said he learned much from her, A couple of months after we started, Bree told him to stop "pushing" the healing, to let it take place in her timing. That gave us something to think about. We are the ones who created time our fixation with it did seem to affect Bree. She was not limited by it and was not concerned by the fact that she was seven years old and not walking. She lived in the present, so she lived in an enlightened state of mind… just a little Buddha. We pay attention to our past and present and so are creating our future. Life got a little easier when I learned to live in Bree's present and not my past and my future.

I had told Marcel about the positive music and cassettes I played during the day for Bree and he came up with the idea of making a tape myself, telling Bree how healthy, strong, and wonderful she was. The sound of the ocean would be the background music and Bree could listen to my voice when she had her afternoon nap and when she went to bed at night. He also came up with the idea of writing about my life with Bree, a scary thought as I had never considered a book and did not know how to write one.

Researchers have declared that by their seventeenth birthday, children have heard one hundred and forty-eight times that they can't do something or other… and of course they can't because it has been programmed into them that they can't. Words that tell them the opposite, that they can do whatever they want to do with the right effort have the opposite effect. I was also using a tape by Caroline Sutherland called "Body Alive" on establishing confidence and self-esteem in children. This is an excellent tape and one I would recommend to all, young and old. For us adults, it is good for the child within us.

Sam lost weight fast. I was away with Bree visiting a friend who lived near Detroit for weeks and was shocked to see him when we returned. I didn't realize how difficult it would be for Sam not having Bree and me around. It was too hot in Toronto during the summer and we decided to get Bree and Sam out of the city. Bree, Sam, and I would go and spend the summer with my parents in the Eastern Township of Quebec and then at the end of the summer, Walter would join us and we would go to the Gaspe for a two week vacation.

Bree had a major seizure a week before we left. Walter had gone upstairs to check on her and he called down, "She looks as if she is praying she's praying." She had crawled out of her bed and was lying near the window. Her off breathing alerted me to the fact that we had a problem and immediately started our usual routine, with Walter masking and applying cold compresses while I massaged her feet and talked to her, Bree took forty minutes to respond and then about half an hour later was still having tremors. It was one-forty in the morning before she settled into a restless sleep. The following morning she slept until eleven-thirty before rousing to take some vegetable juice and rice cream. By one o'clock she was awake and active, behaving like her usual self.

Because of the heat we decided to move down into the basement to sleep. It was at least ten to fifteen degrees cooler than upstairs, which reached ninety degrees.

The seizure forced us to take another look at Bree's diet. She had a tendency to be constipated and Mary told me once my cooking was too "yang" so I added lighter vegetables such as bok choy, Chinese cabbage, more of the leafy greens, seeds, kantans, brown rice vinegar and pressed salads. I felt I was probably refrigerating too many of her foods and I went back to rereading my macrobiotic cookbooks. I found a section in which a nurse working in Belgium had stated that she could not make a sick person well on refrigerated foods.

The trip to my parents' house was stressful as the air conditioner in the car wasn't functioning. The heat of the summer was always a sensitive time for Bree and the possibility of seizure activity increased. This time before my parents left for the Gaspe, she had a major seizure. I called my mother to help me and my father disappeared from the kitchen as this was more than he could handle. It was hard on my mother for she had never seen anyone having a seizure, let alone having to help bring granddaughter out of one. She was so fearful that I had to get stern, telling her that she would have to leave if she didn't control her fears and not voice them out loud which I felt was affecting Bree. It took a little more than an hour for Bree to come out of that one. This incident left quite an impression on my mother and she had an even deeper respect for me and my life journey with Bree.

It was obvious that the heat upstairs was too much for Bree to tolerate even in a small country town. I made makeshift arrangements for her and myself on the big screened-in porch and Sam joined us. It was fun… camping out.

Chapter 14

We intended to go to the Gaspe cabin for three weeks and this meant a lot of advanced planning because the items I needed for macrobiotic cooking were not obtainable in that area, even foods supposedly fresh were far from satisfactory. The idea of leafy greens there was iceberg lettuce from Montreal which was six hundred miles away. My mother had taken a couple bags to save some space in our car and I would have to take enough organic vegetables, grains, beans, and bean products to last for the length of our stay. I spent the entire day prior to our departure in the kitchen cooking food for Bree to have on the road during our drive which would take us almost twelve hours. All the organic food we'd need I had bought the day before in Montreal, a three hour trip from Sutton.

That night, during a talk with my oldest brother, I mentioned we were leaving for the Gaspe the next day and he astonished me by saying that our parents (who had his two children with him) couldn't leave the cabin the next day because it was a holiday in Quebec and the roads would be too busy with traffic for them to drive. They would be driving a total of two hours in Quebec and then be in New Brunswick where the holiday was not celebrated. I greeted his statement coldly. The arrangements had been made two months earlier, all the preparations had been completed, and there was no way I would abandon our plans for such a trivial reason, especially as Walter had to take his vacations at set times and could not alter dates at my brother's selfish whim. I hadn't reckoned with what he would do next. He phoned my parents and told them not to leave. The called us asking that we delayed our vacation.

One of my major issues had been that none of my family, except possibly my mother, ever realized the enormous amount of effort and stress involved in raising a brain-injured child. For the first six-years of her life, Bree had lived in almost constant life-threatening condition with the result that I spent that time making decisions on how best to keep her safe and healthy yet lead as normal a lifestyle as possible. The resultant stress and anxiety this responsibility brought was extremely difficult.

They could make last minute decisions about their children and could, on impulse, decide to eat any greasy spoon that suited them while every move I made had to be calculated beforehand with meticulous preparation...otherwise we ended up paying for it with illness or seizures.

I was quite determined that all our preparations for this trip would not be in vain, so I called my cousin Valerie who lived next door to the cabin and asked if we could spend the night at her place. She agreed with open arms. Our vacation turned out to be a time of mixed emotions. In addition to the problems with my brother, things were even more complicated by the death of my father's sister which necessitated the return of my parents and the arrival of other relatives which caused a reshuffling of living arrangements. This irritated some family members, but we stayed in the cabin.

In addition, we had the burden of knowing that Sam's time with us was drawing to a close. Our sorrow was alleviated somewhat by an understanding relative: eighty-year-old Uncle Cecil. He was a farmer and animal lover and understood what we were going through. He drove Walter back into the woods to some land he owned, so Walter could pick out a beautiful spot where Sam could be buried. It was a hard day when we took Sam to the beach for his last swim and made him a special meal which he could not eat. Walter then took Sam for the last of many walks they had shared. The vet came... it was all over... all too soon!

This vacation was different from previous ones in other ways, too, especially for Walter. He was doing a lot of re-evaluating his work and where he was heading. Instead of windsurfing all day long, he took long canoe rides and went to see my cousins fish for salmon, He was beginning to wonder if the climb up the corporate ladder was worth the effort it demanded.

For some time he had been contemplating a move for us to Vermont and this was becoming more of a possibility. He had contacts in that state and planned to get in touch with a few of them and then see what came up. Bree and I had a macrobiotic appointment in Boston soon after our return home and Walter was back at work. Our ride back home had been a sad home was a sad one with no Sam taking up room in the back seat and poking his head between the front seats to check that all was well.

Our consultation in Boston was well, with some environmental changes being suggested. Dr. Mark Van Cauwenberghe, our consultant this time, raised an interesting point when he asked me how much contact Bree had with male relatives in our families. That made me realize how little there was. The males never talked to her, had never held her, or spent any real time with her. Even Walter's direct contact was minimal time, especially during the period when he was trying to decide whether to move or not. His job took him away from home for at least three months a year.

We decided we would leave Toronto as soon as the opportunity presented itself. We felt we had given the city a fair trial, but it had not lived up to our expectations and we were not happy there. The financial aspect was also a problem. We were barely keeping our heads above water and it didn't look as though we could ever afford to buy a house of our own there. Walter had been having some intermittent chest pains and we were also troubled by air and noise pollution. We just could not envision a permanent future for us in Toronto.

The more I thought about it, the more positive I was that moving to Vermont would be the best answer and it seemed as though things were working towards getting us there. My brother Lynden phoned us to ask if we could store a truck for him for a few days. Seeing this as a sign that we were meant to go, I countered by asking if we could use it to move some of our belongings to store in my parents' house. Moving things to a place that was only a ten-minute drive from the Vermont border where my parents lived would be a step in the right direction.

I had no logical reason for thinking we would definitely be going to Vermont, but something inside told me to act as if we were. I have come to look on these incidents as Spirit guidance. Many years later I read that one of the best ways to change ourselves or our situations is to act as if we are the person we want to be or in the situation we want to be in. Acting in the guidance, I even checked out Vermont papers for rental places. Initially this was a disappointing aspect. Still I felt that if we were meant to move there, the right place would turn up, as would the right job for Walter, so I continued to think and act in a positive manner.

We had a second disappointment when one potential job for Walter didn't work out. However, I just saw this as a sign that he wasn't meant to have that particular position and that a better one would be forthcoming. My mother was amazed at my positive reaction to what she saw as negative forces. I couldn't explain my reaction to her... I knew with certainty that we would be living in Vermont before long, some suitable job would turn up for Walter.

On Monday, September the first, Walter called me from Vermont where he had gone to check out some possibilities. He had the offer of a teaching job. He was qualified to teach at the high school level and about fifteen years earlier he had taught in one for a year. Because he had time to spare before going to an interview he had dropped in to a local high school where he had taught to find out what salary teachers were being paid. Falling back on teaching he had held in reserve in case nothing turned up in the sporting goods business.

Not only did he find out what the salary was, about have of what he earned in Toronto, but that particular school had a vacancy they were trying to fill. It was in special education and when they learned that he was the father of a brain-injured child and therefore had years of experience in the field, they were very anxious to hire him.

I told him the decision was up to him but reminded him that he had left the teaching profession all those years ago because he didn't like it. I didn't want him to go back into it and then find out he had made a mistake.

An hour later he called back to say that there was a place to rent if he decided to take the job and he suggested coming back for me and we could look over the situation together.

The rental was a very small two-bedroom town house with no storage areas or basement. On the plus side, it was clean and only a three-minute walk from the school. It was in the center of the town of St. Albans, so I would be able to walk wherever I needed to go. We decided to rent the house.

We were not without misgivings as we packed up for Vermont. One does not give up a well paying corporate position for an underpaid teaching job without wondering if it is the right choice. By North American standards, what we were doing was totally unbelievable. As money was a problem we decided to hold a garage sale and sell anything we didn't really need. The sale produced a welcomed $300 to our funds.

There was a little uncertainty about whether we would be able to move to the States as a family. We had made inquiries at a border post on an earlier visit and had been told Bree and I would need green cards, those much valued Alien Resident Identification cards that would make us legal, and that sometimes they took a while to process. We were advised to apply as soon as possible. Although Walter was born in Canada, both of his parents were United States citizens so he had dual citizenship and two passports. Moving to the States presented him with no problem. We had three weeks in which to get everything finalized and at the outset we struck a snag. We did not have Bree's original birth certificate and had to send to Quebec for it.

When the day finally came, we set off with our passports in order but without our green cards. We were lucky at the border post to find the same official we had talked with earlier about moving to the States. He got permission from his superior to give us visitor's passes and told us to go to the immigration office in St. Albans the first thing the next morning to set things in motion for our permanent stay.

Our visit to the immigration office didn't go smoothly. The official in charge told me that Bree and I should have remained in Canada until our green cards were issued. He scared me by telling about a woman who had recently been sent back to Canada. He also hinted that the official who had been so helpful at the border might be in trouble because of us.

I was devastated and found myself fighting back tears. This man was so could. I asked him what he expected me to do, go back to Canada and stay in a hotel with a brain-injured child on a special diet and wait while my husband stayed here in the States? (I said a prayer that our helpful friend at the border would not suffer because of his kindness to our family.) We were then presented with a pile of forms to fill in and we were photographed and fingerprinted. I had to get a physical examination and then we were issued temporary resident cards. I was also warned we should not leave the country until our permanent cards were issued. If we did, we would not be let back in. It was just four days before Christmas and we had planned to spend it with Walter's parents, but that plan had to be dropped.

It took three months for me to receive my permanent card, but Bree presented the immigration office with a problem because of her brain-injury. The officials were not quite sure what the procedure was in such case. Her temporary card was extended several times and it was fifteen months before she received her permanent one.

It was fortunate that we did not know ahead of time that Bree's card would take so long to come through for, if we had, we probably would have cancelled our plans for the move. Things, after all, were going our way. According to the law, we should not have been allowed to enter the way we did, but there was a hand involved which was much more powerful than that of the government.

Vermont was a new beginning in many ways. Walter had started eating a macrobiotic diet. There was a fully equipped kitchen at his school, so he was able to take his food each day and heat it up at lunchtime. He enjoyed his work and the people he was working with. The last time he had been so contented was when he was a ski school director.

He and Bree got a chance to spend more time together and things were going well. I loved Vermont. The food supplies I needed were much easier to get there than they had been in Canada and I could have them delivered to our house in no time. I was very impressed by the delivery and postal service in the States. People complained about the postal system but they had never experience the periodic postal strikes we had in Canada… plus a letter taking eight days just to cross the city of Toronto.

Almost all the information I had gathered over the years that had helped me with Bree had come from the United States, so it seemed appropriate to be living in that country now. The larger population and subsequent larger number of people suffering from various problems meant there had been more demand for alternative healing methods and all the books and tapes which I had to order and clear through Customs in Canada were now readily available to me.

St. Albans was a small village compared to Toronto and because of that it was mentally, emotionally, and physically better health-wise. Once a week I went to Burlington, a half-hour drive, to buy our weekly supplies and I found it a pleasure to drive in next-to-nil traffic with beautiful views along the way. Vermont was proving to be all we had hoped for and during the weekly drives, I thanked God for getting us to a place of such beauty and peace.

Chapter 15

Walter's Job involved working with brain-injured children ages fourteen to twenty, teaching them such things as cooking and social skills. He got back to biking and running every day. During the winter months, he assisted the coach of the cross-country ski team and went skiing each day after school.

Having some time for myself was a welcome change. I started taking a sewing class at night once a week during the first winter. The following year I enjoyed some ice skating and cross-country skiing.

We had some ideas about buying a house and setting up something to supplement Walter's income, such as a bed and breakfast, but the problem was that we were living from paycheck to paycheck and finding money for the house seemed like an insurmountable problem. We did, however, spend weekends exploring different areas hoping to see a place where we were like to live permanently.

My parents visited us in the late fall, but my father was in a bad mood from the start and Bree who is affected by the atmosphere around her, picked up on his attitude and was tearful. The situation was so strained that I suggested that my father leave, as he obviously wanted to, and that my mother should stay on for a longer visit. As soon as my father left, everything was fine. Walter watched Bree while Mom and I went window shopping. I drove her around to see the neighborhood.

It as such a relief to be free of the stress my father's presence always created and Mom could relax in a way she wasn't able to do when he was around. My father was a man who needed to be in control at all times. One of the ways he kept my mom on edge was to talk about leaving almost as soon as he arrived. She never felt totally relaxed as she would be pleading to stay an extra day. She would always have to plead to spend time with her children and to play golf. He seemed to enjoy keeping her guessing.

It was on that visit that I noticed my mom's fairly constant cough. I thought it was caused by nervous tension. When she arrived home, she was put on antibiotics.The medicine did not have the desired effect and so she was given a chest x-ray which showed she had fluid in the lungs and she was admitted to the hospital to have the liquid drained. Then, after a series of tests, there came the news she had dreaded for years... she had lung cancer. The prognosis for survival was a mere two months. The doctors wanted to start chemotherapy right away.

I proposed she should go to Boston for a macrobiotic consultation and arranged my appointment. My father and my brother Garth went with us, though my father was not at all interested in Macrobiotics. He sat through the consultation and lectures because of my mother's determination to look into this. Garth was influenced enough by what he heard there to make some changes in his own diet.

Despite their visit to Boston and what they learned there, my father and brother still never questioned anything the doctors in Montreal said about my mother's illness and treatment and they were anxious to return home immediately for further test which had been arranged for her. My feeling was that the tests would not change my mother's condition but only exhaust her.

My father had always prided himself on his ability to cook and my offer to teach him macrobiotic cooking was not well received. He seemed to take any suggestion that he should change his methods as criticism. He did, however, agree to come with Mom and stay with us, but he expected me to show him my methods instantly so he could take over cooking for our household.

From experience I knew only too well that the attitude of the cook had a great influence on what was produced and that it would not do for him to cook for Bree. I believed that his state of almost constant anger and his and his non-recognition of her as a person would affect the quality of the food he was cooking for her. I told him I would do all the cooking for a couple of weeks while he was in the learning process and he reluctantly agreed.

It was hard getting adjusted to having two more people in our small house and to the extra cooking involved. There were the macrobiotic recommendation for Mom which meant two "healing" diets and standard macrobiotic diets for Dad, Walter, and myself. I figured that once I got into the swing of this, I would start cooking classes for Dad and Mom. In the meantime Dad was pushing my mother's sisters had chosen chemotherapy after being diagnosed as having lung cancer and they had both died, so she was understandably reluctant to follow that route.

Mom was weak and in a state of panic but she knew what she wanted to do. During her lifetime she had seldom stood up to my father and now that it really mattered, she found it difficult to assert herself. The situation was frustrating me, watching what was happening and unable to do much about it. I had no desire to interfere between my parents, so all I could do was show them what I knew and then leave them to work things out.

They stayed with us for seven weeks and during that time I made available everything I had in the way of books and videos. My father barely managed to finish one of the books and my mother, though interested, was too easily tired to read much. My father wanted her to show some fighting spirit, but she was dealing with this challenge the same way she had dealt with all resentments... silently. Cancer is known to be a disease related to suppressed resentment and anger. Mom harbored a lot of resentment towards my father which she had never felt free to express. I shall never forget sitting on the couch with her talking about life and she shared with me how much she resented my father's domination. I suggested that she share these feelings with him. She looked at me, eyes wide open, and stated firmly that she could never do that. I knew then that my mother would rather die than speak up and that it was only a matter of time. Years later I would come to realize how hard it is to change the pattern of a lifetime. Two weeks after they arrived my father had acute stomach cramps. I thought it might be associated with the change of diet and prepared a kuzu drink and some mushroom tea for him. He was still in pain, so I prepared a ginger compress to put on on his back, saying that if this treatment was unsuccessful, he would have to go to the hospital. He wanted me to put the compress on his stomach, but I refused because he had acute appendicitis, that would be the worst treatment.

I put a hot towel soaked in ginger on his back over his kidneys. For thirty minutes I was running downstairs to get one hot towel after another. Finally the pain was gone. I said a silent prayer that the emergency was over because caring for Bree and my mom.. and then my father… was almost too much for me to handle. Walter was in New York City for a week-long teachers' convention, making things more hectic than usual. My dad was not good at watching Bree and my mother was too weak to help, so I was looking forward to Walter's return for some relief and support. Friday night at six o'clock there was no Walter. He had promised to be home by then and at nine the phone rang. Walter said he was tied up and would not be home until later. That was the last straw for me. I was exhausted after a week of dealing with all the problems alone. He was having a beer at his boss' house house claiming there were issues to be discussed. My response was direct. "You have a dying mother in law and a brain-injured child, so don't tell me there are more important issues somewhere else!" Walter was home in half an hour.

Once home, Walter admitted that the issue arose because a teacher had made a pass at him. The other male teacher had gone home, but Walter stayed for another beer. He also told me about the week in New York which was pretty much an on-going party, driving around the New York with a case of beer in the car. He said he was sorry for not being fair and told me this was something he never would have admitted a few years earlier.

Mom and Dad were going back home. I could have managed having Mom alone for a longer visit but not my father. I was glad I had been able to return a little of the care and love Mom had given me over the years, but it was not my place to come between the,. Mom was reluctant to return home, but my father was insistent. A week later she was in the hospital having chemotherapy.

What my family were doing... fighting disease with chemicals... was something I had left behind years earlier, but they still regarded doctors' decisions as law, even though they had seen what I had accomplished for Bree with alternative treatment. All the medicines Bree tok to control her seizures had worked to a certain extent, yet they had done nothing to cure them or eliminate what caused them. As a society we have been programmed to take pills for a variety of reasons – to induce sleep, to wake us up, make us happy, give us more energy and so on, but little attention is given to the causes of the problems. For the most part medicines make us feel better temporarily. In the long term, the body needs stronger and stronger doses and only becomes weaker in the process. Often there is either mental, emotional, or spiritual problems involved. True healing takes place when we get to the source of the problem our bodies are reacting to and then and only then can we eliminate it by bringing the body back into balance.

When using medications with Bree, I had never felt in control the way I have since I learned to work with her body through diet and other positive healing alternatives. My most frightening years were the first five when I felt no control over what was happening, depending solely on hospitals and the directions of doctors.

When my mother was discharged from the hospital in June, we visited her and it was obvious she was not being given a healing diet. When I tried to discuss this with my father, he flew into a rage and I realized it was a lost cause and stopped offering information. My mother was aware of what was happening but she was a captive audience to my father... their roles were set and would be played out to the end.

Walter was through school in mid-June and we had arranged to spend one weeks at a macrobiotic summer camp and Great Barrington, Massachusetts. Walter would be working at the camp in the children's program and because of that, Bree and I would be charged a minimal cost. I was looking forward to what would be my first real vacation in years. Every other vacation I had had to cook and clean. At the camp I would not have to cook for a whole week, Just be with Bree and that sounded like heaven to me.

Money was still tight. We were waiting for our tax refund from Canada, relying on it to pay off some of our bills and to buy and air conditioner that we needed for Bree. That was a very hot summer and we spend as much time as possible at Lake Champlain, a five-minute drive from out house. Bree was extremely sensitive to heat which caused seizure activity. Even though I was not keen on air conditioning because it puts the body into and artificially-cooling atmosphere, prevention of seizures seemed more important, so I justified the purchase of one as a security blanket.

When we arrived at the camp, Walter began helping the organizers with preparations. Nextm he worked with the six to ten-year-old children. We had a nice-sized room with a balcony overlooked the trees. We had brought our largest fan and were quite comfortable. It took me a couple of days to adjust to walking up to a counter and selecting healthy meals instead of having to spend hours preparing and cooking them. How wonderful to have a full week ahead of me as well as having a chance to learn a great many new things.

The greatest was going to be having to choose which of the many lectures to attend for there usually were three at a time.

Mary Kett and Suzanne arrived on Monday and it felt good to have my support team there to guide me through the week. Mary sat down with me and pointed out which lectures would be most worthwhile for me.

Walter wasn't interested but was having a great time working with the children and we met for lunch. I took Bree to the lectures with me and put her down for a nap when the afternoon lectures were over. Walter suggested that I leave Bree with the youngest children for one of the lectures, so I could have some time to myself. I knew she would not require any special attention for one and a half hours… the length of time I left her with a dry bottom and a favorite toy. I also knew all the little children were immobile and kept in a safe place.

When I went to make arrangements for leaving Bree, I was shocked to get a flat rejection, despite my assurance that Bree would be no trouble. It felt like a slap in the face. Once again, my little girl was being rejected for no reason except fear on the part of the caregivers in the tots program. I guess I expected more of them because they were practicing the macrobiotic way of life. I went back to our room and cried for half an hour.

Instead of leaving Bree, I took her to the next class which was on wild food. We were seated under a tree with branches so wide and so low they completely hid us. We were told to close our eyes and get a feel for the tree itself, to listen to it and to receive impressions from it. My impressions came hard and fast as I thought about my morning's experience. Here was this tree that had been taken for granted over the years, with people cutting its branches and swinging from them without really appreciating it. For me it was a symbol of man's ignorance of this environment, his indifference to God's gifts. We were asked a little later to verbalize our impressions, but mine had affected me so badly I could not speak at first but did later. I felt I had had experienced "being one with nature."

The week as a whole was a wonderful experience. The two subjects that fascinated me the most were the study of wild foods and learning about dowsing. I decided to explore more about these subjects in the future. David Yarrow taught the dowsing class and I wrote down the address of the Dowsing Association which happened to be in Vermont. I learned there was to be an annual convention the following September. It would be in Danville, an hour and a half drive from St. Albans. I would not be able to attend the two-day school or the full week of lectures, not having anyone to take care of Bree but I could at least go for the last day, a Saturday when Walter could take care of her. I hoped to learn some interesting information and it should be a beautiful ride through the Green Mountains on a lovely fall day.

One interesting thing I learned when I had lunch with David Yarrow at the convention dealt with information gathered over the years about the prevalence of cancer and other illnesses in houses that were built over a crossing water vein. Research on this subject had been going on for thirty years in Germany. The study had shown that a high percentage of cancer cases, as high as ninety percent, occurred in houses where a crossing vein ran under the patient's bed. David mentioned that he had checked out the houses of eleven cancer-stricken people that Mary Kett knew and found that seven of them had water veins crossing under their beds. Research in the United States has only been going on for six years and was nowhere near as extensive as that done in Germany, but information coming from it is interesting, to say the least.

Walter's reaction to this information was, "Why no get David Yarrow to check out your mother's house?" I contacted David and he agreed to check my Mom's house. I warned him that my dad would not be interested. However, my mother was keen to have it done and her welfare was my main concern.

David dowsed all around the house and grounds. It took all afternoon. He found a major water column running under the dining room with seven veins fanning out from it. He found a vein that flowed under her bed and, at a deeper level, a major flow of sixty gallons per minute that passed under her chest level when she was sleeping. I had not told him on which side of the bed she slept nor that the cancer cells were in her lungs. Hu suggested a couple of places where it would be safer for sleeping, but in general, it was not a good house to live in from a dowser's point of view.

During two different summers Walter, Bree, and I had stayed at my parents' home and now I was curious about something. I asked David to dowse under the bedroom that had been ours but I didn't tell home it had been ours or why I wanted it done. Actually, I wanted to know if there was a water column under it and, if so, where it was in relation to the place we have put Bree's futon. It was interesting to find that Bree's head had been right on top of a water column… and last time she had a long seizure had occurred when she had been sleeping in that room. It seemed to me that the ingredients that caused the seizure had been the full moon, the hot summer's night, and sleeping over a water column, a combination severe enough to trigger an explosion in anyone who was highly sensitive.

It seemed obvious to me that I should learn more about dowsing, to acquire Earth knowledge, in an attempt to be in tune with the Earth and working on it.

Mom was very much interested in what David was doing. From her bed on the porch, she watched with keen interest as we dowsed the front yard. I loved looking back at her as she stretched her neck to watch with a twinkle in her eye. True to form, my father was disinterested to the point of being rude. If he didn't understand something, he couldn't take control, so it was of no value as far as he was concerned.

That evening I received a phone call from my mom. She was sad and exhausted. She said she had just been through a scene with my father, asking him to place her bed in one of the safe areas that David had recommended and that he had raged all through doing this for her. Mom could not talk further because my father walked into the room and would not leave. I wanted to much to help her, but they had been married almost fifty years and they had to work their problems out. To me, Mom was a caged bird who wasn't even allowed to sing!

Twelve days later, my mother was dead.

My brother Richard had called to let me know that she was in the hospital and would undergo radiation as her condition had worsened, but when I called her doctor, he said it was not necessary for me to rush to Montreal. He gave her another month at least. Early the next morning Richard called to say that she was slipping away fast. My father had been summoned to the hospital at 5 a.m. I told Richard I would be there as soon as possible.

After preparing food for Bree to have while I was away, I left as soon as Walter got home from teaching school. It was a long hour and a half drive to Montreal and I kept sending mental messages to Mom to hang in until I got there. When I arrived she was still alive but very weak. As soon as she saw me, she gave me a look that said, "Get me out of here, Wen," and I burst into tears. The intensive care cardiac ward was cold and sterile and the nurses seemed impersonal. I felt intimidated by all the machinery. I told Mom how much I loved her that she was a wonderful mother… yet she wanted out and I could not do anything.

I left her so my father or brother could see her as we were only allowed to see her one at a time. Five minutes later, she was dead. She was alone when she died and I regret that I allowed the intensive care procedure to cloud my thinking. I wish that I climbed in bed with her and held her in my arms. The one thing I said to her before I had left was, "Mom, just keep on calling Jesus. Remember the time you felt a hand on your shoulder when you were alone. He has always been there for you when your have been afraid."

Mom died at 7:30 p.m. When I went back in to see her body, there was only the framework. My mother had moved on.

I was the only one of my siblings who could stay with my father that night. He had shown me no sympathy or understanding about Bree and I felt it was ironic that I should be with him the first night after the death of his wife of over fifty years! We had little to say to each other. He wandered around the house until four in the morning looking at Mom's things, calling me to show me something or other. I stayed up watching television until six as I was unsure how he would react. As much as he demanded independence, he was bound to be a little lost at such a traumatic time.

It was extremely stressful for me as well and I managed to get only eleven hours of sleep during my four-day stay. Family members gathered from British Columbia and Nova Scotia and one of my brothers was there. Other family members were nearby. It might be the last time for us all to be together because it was my mother who had kept the family together.

Losing my mother was a great blow to me for she was the only family member who had supported me one hundred percent in my efforts with Bree. Many times she had clipped articles that might be of interest or use. She always checked on how we fared in Philadelphia or Boston. Her love of unconditional and Bree knew it.

That fall I found a store called "What An Interesting Bookstore." It was well named and I spent time there searching for books that feed me emotionally and spiritually. Dowsing had introduced me to "Feng Shui," which was the Chinese art of placement. Chinese tradition held that there were placements of houses and furniture that were conducive to health and well-being... one could change the "chi" energy of a house by the use of wind chimes, plants, and mirrors. The Chinese had been working with their methods for thousands of years and it made sense to me. I had felt good in certain places, uncomfortable in others, as many people do, without realizing why.

The last thing Mom had supported me in was testing a sample of Bree's hair for food allergies. The sample was sent to England and the results showed she was allergic to fish, dairy foods, sugar, sunflower, corn, and wheat. When I took these foods out of her diet and gave her remedies that were recommended, her seizure activity diminished drastically. Within weeks, Bree was more active and vocal and she became much stronger as the winter progressed.

I was feeling very tired during that period, suffering from an emotional adjustment to Mom's death. I came to the realization that I needed to pay more attention to my own health. The Biblical expression, "Physician, heal thyself," became very real to me. I had always focussed my full attention on Bree, not comprehending how much my own state of health was tied in with hers.

Spiritually and emotionally, Bree was more advanced than I could possibly hope to attain in my lifetime. She was incapable of a negative thought and therefore lived in a state of grace that automatically made her very special in this world.

The new year brought many changes, one of which was the commencement of this book. The thought of writing this book about Bree was scary, as I did not have any writing experience. I had lived the story but did not know whether I could get my message across to other parents and to those who knew or worked with a brain-injured child. How could I get them to understand how truly precious the gift of a child like Bree is?

Brain-injured children are our guides and teachers. It is not the other way around. I hoped that people would understand that having a brain-injured child was not just a matter of survival, but something for which to give thanks. Would I be able to get this message across?

I started writing at night, my only free time, although I was having a discussion with Walter about having more time for myself. To put it simply, I wanted to have the same amount of free time as he had. The way it was right then, he would spend his free time skiing and then wanted to get a sitter to give me some free time… while he got even more time for himself. The alternative, as he saw it, was for him to spend time cross-country skiing, for example, and then spend time in the ski hut, then I would get to ski. In actuality, that meant I ended up looking after Bree while he skied and during family time, I ended up looking after Bree. I wanted some time totally for myself to go skiing alone in the woods or ice skating at the arena five minutes from our house. I did start skating at 6:30 in the morning while Bree and Walter were asleep. I had been skating from early childhood and don't even remember learning. Skating is a form of meditation for me, a chance to think of nothing, nothing at all…

How wonderful it was when I finally started getting some time to myself. This was a first for me, as everything I had been doing was for the family. Even the sewing lessons I took were to learn how to make clothes for Bree. Now I was spending time alone doing something just for myself.

I was still calling Marcel Vogel every other Wednesday, drawing inspiration from our conversations, but one Wednesday morning his son answered. He told me his father had died of a heart attack the previous Sunday. I felt a tremendous sense of loss. Marcel had become a very positive father-figure to me. He had connected better with Bree than anyone else I knew and it was difficult to accept the fact that I would never hear his voice again!

With the gift of more time for myself, I was slowly beginning to heal emotionally. It dawned on me that during the past eight and a half years, I had been living in a state of panic, constantly doing things for others without taking time to nourish myself... to meet my own needs. And I began to like myself, this person called Wendy.

Walter had always been able to remove himself from the situation, sleeping soundly even if Bree was sick. I couldn't do that. Now that she was stronger, I could leave her for short periods and not feel there would be a price to pay. Before it had not made much sense to take superficial free time if it meant coming back to a sick child and having to spend a couple of weeks repairing the damage that had been done.

We were to return to the macrobiotic camp that summer, but this time I was taking a sitter with me so I would be able to attend lectures without Bree. This would make the week much more enjoyable for both of us. It was not much fun for her to sit through long lectures although she had been super about it. In the meantime, I was still reading a great deal and searching for answers and alternatives. I was a very good customer at What An Interesting Bookstore.

Walter's first job in St. Albans ended because of cut-backs and he found a job teaching in a high school in Enosburg Falls, which was about a half hour commute. He worked with dysfunctional children. He didn't want to work too far away and so he accepted a position he didn't like and that almost doomed it from the start. The teenagers "bugged" him for the first month and he didn't get along well with his boss. This was the beginning of two years of conflict between the,... with Walter giving me a running commentary each night about all the day's disasters.

Our relationship was deteriorating and, at the end of August, I told him I did not want to continue our marriage. I was forty and wanted to have another child. My biological clock was ticking, or should I say "booming"! He did not want to have another child and he and had a vasectomy when Bree was two years old. Soon afterwards he agreed to and international adoption but six months into the paperwork, he told me to forget it because he did not want anymore children, international or otherwise. I felt so alone in my marriage. Walter lost interest in Bree when the stimulation program did not make her totally well. He said he would leave if I continued to do the stimulation program when he was at home. Bree was my life in that everything I did was to keep her alive, healthy, and happy. Now I had to decide my future. We no longer shared a common dream.

In December a call came from Montreal Children's Hospital. A doctor was doing research on children with Bree's syndrome who had lived into a second decade. Two others had been found in Canada and they wanted to do tests on all three. We agreed, providing the tests would be done at our house, as we were not prepared to take her to the hospital unless absolutely necessary. They had only found a few others in North America with Wolf-Hirschhorn Syndrome, the oldest being fourteen. Bree was eleven then and the only one who was totally free of medications. She had not had any for over five years and was the healthiest of all the children. They were impressed but had difficulty attributing the results I had achieved to stimulation, nutrition, and a positive environment. One doctor did admit that he had heard of someone having fantastic results with Chinese herbs but as a doctor, it was difficult for him to accept all this without controlled studies.

Walter and I were still living together, sharing the rental as housemates until we could afford separate homes. Bree was a happy, healthy, twelve-year-old… my pride and joy. How I wish Walter could see what a wonderful individual she was, but he had trouble making any connection with her and he no longer took any responsibility for her. He flatly refused to listen to anymore of what her termed "metaphysical bullshit." He saw Bree as taking from his life while I saw her as adding immeasurably to mine. Sharing space is as far as our togetherness went.

Chapter 16

Divorce had become the only solution for our different points of view. This saddened me because I believe in marriage and honor family life, yet Walter and I could no longer find common ground and I knew complete separation was paramount for my peace of mind. I had been working in a bookstore on Saturdays for seven months. The store was for sale and if things had been ideal, money would have appeared from somewhere and I would have been able to buy it. That was just a dream. It would have required a solid financial base to support it, myself, and Bree, as well as a live-in caretaker to work on Bree's stimulation program. Buy the store was out of the question.

But what could I do to support Bree and myself? Where could I go? I had no idea how we could manage and yet I started packing to leave. I even had a yard sale to get a little money and get rid of things I could not take with me. As I packed, I kept praying for some sort of a sign that would give me an answer to my program.

My mother had told me, about three years before she died, that she had arranged a separate amount of money, about $15,000, that was to go to Bree. When I asked my father about this, he said there was no such money and he did not offer any kind of help. There were no offers from any family members or friends. I felt abandoned. Once again it was my faith that kept us going until a door would open. That is when I wrote the first draft of this story as I just kept packing. I would plead for insights and all the guidance I received was to clean out another closet or to pack up the kitchen stuff. How frustrated and frightened I was!

The first week of August of 1992, Bree and I went to another macrobiotic summer conference and my girlfriend Susie went with me to help with Bree. At this point Walter still worked at the conference, so we were able to attend at no cost. Little did I know that an incident would occur at the conference that would lead to a solution to my problems and that Bree would be the one to start the ball rolling.

The summer conference was a place where I found connection. These people were living the same lifestyle as we were. Half-way through the week, I decided to take Bree to a music and dance workshop. I knew she would enjoy that. During the break while I was talking to the man who led the class, Bree was busy holding another man's finger. He name was Will Tuttle, a pianist who was part of the entertainment. She had such a firm grip that I asked Will if she was hurting him. He said she wasn't, so I continued talking with the instructor.

Bree and I left the class a bit early, so I could prepare her lunch. Will left with us. I thought he was just helping me with the door, but he continued walking with us. He turned out to be our angel in disguise. Although I had no idea that he would be the one to start opening important doors for me, Bree must have known for she was the one who got his attention while I was involved in conversation.

After the conference Will and I kept in touch. Some time later that fall, while I was still trying to find a way out of my dilemma, we were having a phone conversation when he mentioned that his mom could use a house-mate for the winter. Years later he told me how unusual it had been for him to suggest anything like this. He is a Buddhist and he was sure it was spiritual guidance that led him to the choice. Will was very productive of his mother, Beverly, and because he traveled a great deal around the country playing his music, he wanted to be sure she would have no problems. He didn't know me well. What if it didn't work out? That's why it took guidance to make his decisions. And so Bree and I were headed for life in New Hampshire.

On the eleventh November I crossed the Green Mountains hauling a five by eight-foot trailer with a severely brain-injured twelve-year old ... with a place to stay for only four months. How did I get the courage to do this? I had no other offers and I felt the Spirit did the driving and Bree kept me focused. Marcel Vogel told me that Bree was my spiritual Geiger counter.

Bev Tuttle lived in Danbury, a very small town with one little corner store where one could buy gas. The post office still had combinations on everyone's box, something I had not seen since I was a child. The house was in the middle of the woods and I had never been so har away from anyone I knew and with so much responsibility. Bree was no worried for she felt we were surrounded by a host of angels. I had lived in small towns for the most of my life, but usually there was a neighbor I could call on. Now every person I knew was a long distance telephone call away and I didn't have the money needed to phone them. Meeting my financial commitments was a struggle. Keeping in touch with family and friends was out of the question. I did my Tai Chi practice early each morning while Bree was still sleeping, cared for her though the day, and spent evenings in front of the fireplace with a good book. Bev was an active person and away from home a lot. When she was there, I had a crackling fire going to welcome her home. She told me the fireplace had been little used before I came there.

My lifeline that winter was going back to Burlington for my Tai Chi class. I would get my shopping done there. Burlington had an excellent co-op where I could get organic food. It seemed as if that winter there was a major snowstorm every Saturday night, but Bree and I were guided home safely every time.

The Tuttles became my family. Bev was a second mom, a true godsend, kind and warm hearted. She prayed a lot for Will to become a Christian. He didn't feel he needed her prayers for he felt spiritually guided. What a privilege it has been to have such a wonderful adopted family!

Sometime that winter I called Lee pattison in Australia as she had sent me the edited version of my book and I needed to touch base with her. During our conversation I mentioned how lonely I was feeling and she shared a visual impression she had of me.

"You remind me of those balloons with the lead bottoms which we used to punch as a child to make them fall over, but they always came back up. We would try to give them a really good bump, thinking this would make them stay down, but low and behold, they would bounce back up with even stronger force. Like them, you are always bouncing back!" Then she added, "Think about this Wendy. If you have known twelve years ago what lay ahead of you, you would have probably said. 'No Way!' And year look at all you have made it through."

Yes, I would be able to handle the loneliness. Now I see that time in the woods as a gift. It was a place to hibernate and be safe. It amazes me how we are always being cared for.

Bev's second son, Ed, was coming for a visit. His arrival time at the airport conflicted with an appointment of her which had been scheduled. I offered to pick him up, a small service I could offer her. Bree and I went to the airport. I greeted him with a hug, something I had never done with a stranger. I drove him to his sister's house in Vermont to meet his mother and Will. Will and Ed were like brothers to me. If there is such a thing as reincarnation, then I had met them in a previous lifetime. Just at a time when I was going through a divorce and felt lonely, living in a place where I knew nobody, these two friends arrived. I think an urgent call went into the angel realm and old soul friends showed up to comfort me. At the end of four months Bev left to take a position in Philadelphia. I believe she would have put her house on the market but for me. Where could I go? She offered to lease the house to me. As I had nowhere else to go, I decided to see if I could swing it by getting house-mates to share the expenses. This I did for almost two years.

How I struggled to get people willing to live in such a remote area. And I was so lonely! Finally the situation was too difficult for me to handle. Also, I knew Bev wanted to sell the house. But what to do? Where to go?

I started looking for somewhere to live. What I found were small apartments, two rooms with wall-to-wall carpeting which Bree was allergic to. This was very discouraging.

During my time in Danbury, I did some of my food shopping at a small health food store in the town of New London. I would ask questions of the employees about resources in the area. I had learned over the years that good places to get information about the area were bookstores and health food stores.

One of the employees at the New London health food store was a man named Peter. What impressed me about him was his interest in Bree. He treated her as an interesting person, not as an oddity. This was so refreshing to me. Bree loved this kind of attention. She had had very little experience of being around males that accepted her for herself. Isn't that what all of us want?

Peter and I had started dating, but then I called it off. He was great with Bree but not good for me because I couldn't handle his mood swings. He called me up a while later and asked me to go with him to a group meeting called Open Hearted Listening. He said it was about couples learning to communicate better, so I said I would and we could try again. The meetings were held once a week.

Within a month it was time for the summer macrobiotic conference. Walter was attending for the last time. He called and asked me if I knew of anyone who would work in the children's program. I asked Peter if this was something that would interest him and he said it would. That week gave him the opportunity to see what a macrobiotic lifestyle was all about.

Peter had a small apartment above a garage in New London. He told me there was a place next to his that was being renovated and he thought we could rent it. He could visualize us living there and he talked to the owner. Low and behold, there was a large three-bedroom main floor apartment that seemed ideal. It was on the main street and I would be able to walk with Bree everywhere, yet it was a small town. There was a lot of space with hardwood floors, ideal for Bree to creep around. From the back of the apartment was a view of Mt. Sunapee. It seemed perfect for our needs. Peter wanted to rent it with us as there was no way I could afford it by myself.

Peter's mood swings confused and worried me. He could change from the most loving, charming man I had ever met to a moody, mean person. I attended AA meetings with him and started reading books on alcoholism. At one meeting I shared my concern about Peter's mood swings with a woman who told me that once a person has stopped drinking, it takes five years to really get sober and then another five years to know what to do with that sobriety. What a discouraging statement!

Peter was the only friend I had at that time and I needed a friend. Our relationship had problems, but we could at least try. God had these three lonely people who needed each other.

About a year after our divorce, Walter remarried. When I went to Montreal to visit my brother Garth, which I did about twice a year, I would leave Bree with her father. Walter always seemed a bit put out about having her. He would complain if it didn't suit his schedule. It was as if he were doing me some great favor. This really hurt me because Walter showed no interest in spending time with his daughter. We were divorced, but he did not divorce Bree!

Bree always came back sick. I became concerned because I noticed an increase in the amount of alcohol present in Walter's house. He was in the habit of having a beer daily, but when I opened the refrigerator at his house, there was a two-liter box of wine beside his usual beer and on the counter were a number of bottles of hard liquor. This worried me. Was there a tie-in between the increased amount of alcohol and the fact Bree was sick at the end of her visits? Later I found out Walter's wife was a smoker, a fact Walter had never shared with me. He knew Bree was very allergic to smoke. I reached the conclusion I would no longer ask Walter to care for Bree.

What made me heartsick about the situation was how Walter could turn away from his own daughter. When she was about eleven, he could see that, no matter how much stimulation she received, she could never walk or talk and he appeared to lose interest in her at that time. How could Walter spend eleven years with her and then basically write her off? What I considered the most important event in my life, the birth of Bree, was for him the worst. I knew that if anything ever happened to me, I could not count on him to care for Bree in the manner that I have. Bree is as much a part of Walter as she is of me, yet he could live his life without any concern for her. I wanted him to see what a lovely daughter he has and to be proud to be her father. This type of thinking always brought me on tears and feelings of devastation and I asked myself again and again, "How can a father not care about a daughter and her well being?"

Finally I reached the conclusion that Watler just wanted a way out. His job is working as a coordinator for families with brain-injured children in the public school system. He wants to be able to say that he still has contact with his daughter. Walter asked to visit Bree on her sixteenth birthday. This was unusual for he had not visited her on any other of her birthdays. The day came. I remember so clearly sitting and watching the two of them on the couch. He would periodically pat her on her head, like he used to pat our dog Sam. Bree get trying to get his attention. I had to point this out to him. He showed so little interest in her.

What I found out during that visit was that Walter's wife was taking a course once a month in Hanover, just twenty-five minutes away. She had been taking the course for quite a while and this was her last time, the only one when Walter had asked to see Bree.

Chapter 17

Not long ago I was told that New Hampshire is one of the better states for brain-injured children because the state does not support institutions anymore. This must be just a political front for it certainly was not my experience. Many institutions have been closed down and that is good, but I haven't found that parents are supported in caring for their children at home. I have fought this situation. I am a very self-motivated and focused person. What about parents who don't fight? How do they manage? I have to believe that they give up. The only type of support readily available to me was where the care of Bree would be given to someone else. I could have nurses and other types of caregivers come to the house provided I went to work. The school department in New London was ready to put Bree in an institution called Crotched Mountain.

One day while I was getting my hair done, I shared my story with the hairdresser. She told me her sister had worked at Crotched Mountain once and had left. I asked if she could get her sister to phone me so I could ask her some questions. Her sister said that there was no one-on-one care given at Crotched Mountain and that there were two children in each room… that it was more or less a hospital-type setting. Some of the information she gave me was very disturbing. I decided to visit and see for myself. The building is on the top of a mountain in an isolated area. I went in and knocked on the door of the general information office. I explained that I had some questions and the woman there was very helpful. "Do you have an allergy-free environment?" Was my first question.

The answer I received was, "Yes, we do have children with allergies." That was not what I wanted to know.

"What are your beds likes? Are natural fibers and woods used? And what about carpets?" Beds and carpeting can be the worst offenders for people with allergies. I also asked about the care givers. "Do any of them smoke? Do they use hair sprays perfumes?" The woman had no idea what I was talking about. She only knew that children with allergies were treated with medication. I knew I could never send Bree there.

In June of 1996 I approached the local school department with a request for an aid to come into my home on a daily basis to supplement the work I do with Bree. This is the type of service I had in Vermont. Bree had just turned sixteen and I phoned the district office knowing any action would take time and my hope was that the matter could be resolved before September and the start of the school year. On the fifteenth I dropped off a packet of information. I had been very clear in my telephone conversation with the Special Education Director that a program be set up to take place in my home. I stressed that Bree has both food and environmental allergies.

The information I dropped off was to make the special education staff be more aware of our situation. There was my certificate at the qualified level from the Institutes for the Achievement of Human Potential, a typed Individualized Education Plan (I. E. P.) from my point of view concerning Bree's mental and physical health goals, intellectual and social development, four pages of resource information, and a couple of pages explaining why were were eating macrobiotically. There were also letters from Bree's osteopath, doctor, and physical therapist explaining why they all recommended an I. E. P. that would be carried out in our home, and finally I included an article from the Earth Pulse Magazine called "Kids and Chemicals and Our Schools."

When I have my first meeting with the special education team who were to evaluate Bree and makeup her I. E. P., I learned that the teachers had not seen nor been instructed to review this information. This first meeting took place on August 28, 1996. The next meeting to review the evaluation summary and eligibility for special education services did not take place until December the second, six months from my original request. Bree at sixteen was obviously a totally dependent child and yet the school system delayed any action by indicating that she was still being evaluated. Once I became aware of their delaying tactics, I contacted my area agency, Community Bridges, and asked them to support us at all future meetings with the school system.

On February 12, 1997 I wrote to the Director of Special Education, Marie Wolfe, asking for a draft of the proposed I. E. P. Then in March, I wrote again clarifying position on why a home-based program was vital for Bree. I included information based on interviews with twenty-five distinguished medical doctors from a books by Gary Null, PhD. I quoted case after case where theses doctors had found that mental and physical conditions were associated with specific nutritional deficiencies, an inability of the body to absorb certain nutrients from food. I once again tried to clarify to the Special Education Department the importance of having a home-based program set up for Bree.

On March 27, 1997 the Placement Team from the school district, led by Marie Wolfe, met at my home. My Region 4 advocate was there to support my position because I felt I needed backup. At this I. E. P. meeting I was outnumbered as there were seven school employees. It's somewhat similar to being in a hospital with a room full of doctors talking their unique language when you want to hear in English what concerns the welfare of your child. In both instances they act like the most important element in the child involved, yet to me it was about saving face. I was glad my support person arrived early, so we could talk and be prepared for the meeting.

I felt at ease with all the teachers for they had been to the house at one time or another to evaluate Bree. They all were charmed by Bree and liked working with her. The person I did not have much confidence in was the Director. The first thing I was told was that Bree was eligible for special education. Then they went through everything they would offer, saying that this program had to be carried out at Crotched Mountain! I told them what I had learned about the environment there and the problems it would cause Bree. It did not good. I was wasting my breath.

Marie Wolfe told me how the team, herself, and the teachers had struggled with the decisions of placement. I looked around at the faces of the teachers and could see they were doing what they had to do as employees. These were mothers who have been in my home and I knew they supported me, but they were caught in the middle. I knew the decision was Marie Wolfe's and that of her boss. When she told me the answer was Crotched Mountain, I said that was an insult. She looked at me with a questioning look and said she did not see how it could be an insult. I explained to her that a mother who has worked for seventeen years to keep her daughter alive, happy, and healthy only to be told she should be put in an institution naturally felt grossly insulted. It would be like telling her she should put her eleven-year old daughter in an institution. Then I tried to explain to her about my impression of Crotched when I visited there and also about the disquieting rumors I had heard. I was amazed that her reaction was to tell me about the nice pool they had an the great computer room. Bree wouldn't be able to use the pool because of her allergy to the chemicals it used for purification... and the computer room! What good would a computer be for a child who could neither read nor write. Could a computer replace a loving home environment? I added that I would not accept this decision and that my next step would be mediation.

I knew members on the town council and they recommended that I get in touch with the School Board. I signed the papers to start mediation and sent the following list of reasons why I would only accept a home-based program:

1. Bree has food and environmental allergies. Her allergic reactions trigger petit and grand mal seizures.
2. Bree's seizures have been controlled through a macrobiotic diet and an allergy-free environment which can only be provided in her home.
3. Bree is apt to be constipated and her daily bowel movements are facilitated by Mom with the help of suppositories. Success can only be accomplished by her Mom. (Others have tried without results.)

4. Bree has adverse reactions (seizures) to immunization shots and so has had none since she was a year old.

5. Bree also has adverse reactions (seizures) to antibiotics and has not had any in the last eleven years. Also she has been off all seizure medication for eleven years which has been achieved through a macrobiotic diet and an allergy-free environment.

6. The emotional trauma placed on Bree if she were removed from home is unthinkable. The placement of the I.E.P. at Crotched Mountain is abusive considering that Sandy Hunt, one of the members of the Special Education Team, found Bree's functional level to be below the twelve-month level, according to the Carolina Curriculum for Handicapped Infants and Children at Risk.

7. Crotched Mountain does not provide a macrobiotic diet or an allergy-free environment, according to Debra Flanders, Director of Admissions.

Bree was born with Wolf-Hirschhorn (HP-), an uncommon condition. Seizures are a major concern for parents of children with HP-. Almost all patients with this problem suffer from seizures which range from mild to absence (petit mal) to tonic-clonic (grand mal). Bree to this day still has the grand mal variety and especially if taken into a non-safe environment… for example, a non-macrobiotic way of life that is not allergy-free. Her present level of wellbeing and happiness has only been achieved through years of study and research by her mother who has maintained a lifestyle that quite literally kept her alive. Bree is the only child with tonic-clonic seizures who is medicine-free. This is important because these children are prone to kidney disorders and seizure medications are draining on the kidney.

I sent these reasons to explain why Crotched Mountain was not a viable solution. Then I got in touch with members of the School Board. Within days after these telephone calls, Marie Wolf phoned to say they would like to work with me.

Amazing! It seemed to me that they had wanted to find out just how long I would keep on. The school system wanted to put Bree in a particular slot with no concern about what was best for her. It didn't make sense from a financial point of view. It would cost $120,000 a year for her at Crotched Mountain compared to the $15,000 I was asking. The only way I could figure out the financial picture was that the expense would not be on the local school budget but some state budget.

I met with Marie Wolf and Sandy Hunt from the Special Education Department on May 5, 1997 to discuss the next steps toward getting a program started. By June 16 nothing was underway and so I called a member of the School Board. On the 20th I received a call from Special Education saying that services would begin Monday the 23rd. One year to get Bree what was her legal right and I had to fight tooth and nail to get it! I felt it was my duty to attempt to help other parents felt a better shake than I had and so I wrote to the governor explaining in detail my problems with the Special Education Department. My response from the governor was very supportive. I took her letter to the last School Board June of '97. Presenting my "case" to the School Board was something I dreaded as I have always been very nervous about speaking in front of a group. The old voices from my childhood saying, "You are to be seen but not heard!" and "What makes you think you deserve…" were playing havoc with my thinking, but I would do almost anything that would help Bree. Also, I was doing it in the hopes that I could help smooth the way for other parents of brain-injured children.

I went to the meeting with my typed statement in hand. My heart was in my throat when I got up to make my presentation. I explained that I was nervous. Then I read my statement and the letter from the governor… and left.

August 6. I still had not heard from the School Board and so I called the Chairman of the Board, Dean Bensley. He said he had sent me a letter which I had not received. When I did get the letter, I was informed that a subcommittee of the Board was going to review the Special Education evaluation. And that, due to the summer schedule, they would probably not have any conclusions until the fall.

By March of 1998, I still had received no answer from the School Board about their findings. On March 3rd I went to another Board meeting and requested some form to follow up. An article about Bree and me appeared on March 10th in the Intertown Record, a local newspaper. The paper reported that a mother of a special education student had asked the School Board to respond to her request that they look into the timeliness of testing, that she had approached the Board and the Administration but received no response.

Finally on March 19th I received a letter of apology for the delays, delays for almost two years!

From this experience I learned a great deal about how parents might just give up the struggle. This situation reminded me about the problems I had in dealing with the medical profession. My bottom line when everything appears confusion is that I am the only one who has to answer in the end. If my daughter gets sick, I am the one who stays up all night or all week and not a professional person. No one else was there to come to my aid during the years of struggling to keep Bree alive. I have worked hard to maintain Bree's health and happiness. I will not risk losing ground for anything.

Chapter 18

I walked into a room and Bree was not there. Where was she? I looked around for her in panic. Where could she be? A strange man entered the room and said he would look for Bree. I searched the hotel where we were staying. No Bree! We were attending a seminar that I was giving. Suddenly the man was back. He had found Bree just before she was going to be put on a train, as if she could find her way alone on the train! I woke up. Thank God it was just a bad dream. My fears for our future were invading my dreams. I did not know how I would be about to support Bree and myself when she turned nineteen. Then Welfare would consider Bree to be an independent adult adult and I was supposed to be getting a job, It was a Catch 22 situation and I could see no way out.

Another major problem facing me was that Walter felt that now Bree was over eighteen years old, he should no longer have to pay child support. He told me I had better get used to going without a car because he was not planning on renewing the lease on my car or getting me another one. What should I do? My first step was to get a legal aid lawyer. It seemed as if I was either in tears due to the inhuman way the school department was treating my situation or in tears due to Walter's insensitivity. Not one of the people involved with these issues would be willing to walk in my shoes, day by day for nineteen years!

It took a year to get the finances straightened out with Walter because, in some strange way, he felt his responsibilities were over and he could walk away. He obviously did not give a damn how I would manage without a car and child support. I had an excellent woman lawyer, a mom, who kept me on track when I dissolved into tears or felt afraid to answer the telephone, fearing it might be Walter again, saying I had better get ready to do without a car. My lawyer kept telling me to have Walter call her, When I followed that advice, she handled the situation beautifully. She was not afraid to tell him off and she knew the New Hampshire laws.

About six weeks before a court date, Walter got a lawyer and matter moved faster as it was one lawyer talking with another. I think things got settled because Walter's lawyer let him know that it would probably work better to settle out of court than to have me walk into the courtroom carrying Bree. In the settlement Walter is responsible for leasing a car to me and paying for the registration and insurance. He sent me a check to my food store and one to my landlord, but my allowance stayed the same. This settlement cannot be changed unless there is a written agreement between us and we go back to court. Bree will always be a dependant child and Walter and I will be responsible for her in our individual ways. What had been a stumbling block for me was that I wanted Water to be as concerned about Bree's welfare, health, and happiness as I, something that is not to be. Now I realize the important point is for him to do his share of financial support. Perhaps he is doing his best by meeting his financial responsibilities.

While Bree's support was in question, Walter called her once a week and asked to see her, something he had not done in a long time. I realized this was because he wanted to look good for the judge. Since the settlement, he calls much less frequently. This saddens me, but I have no control over the situation.

The day that Bree turned nineteen she would be considered an adult by Welfare and we would receive no more health coverage or financial help even though I would still be a single mom with a totally dependant daughter which meant that I had less than a year to figure out how I could support us. My allowance from Walter was an insufficient amount. How could I possibly cope? What was I to do?

While I was trying to resolve this problem, my father had to be put in a nursing home. Before this, I had mentioned to my siblings that I thought his memory was slipping. They all said that was just Dad being Dad, so I let it go. I would visit him whenever I went to see my brother Garth in Montreal which was about twice a year. Dad seemed to take more interest in Bree than he had in the past. Several times I noticed Bree staring very intently at her grandfather. I knew that he was very lonely, yet he had driven away people by his difficult nature. In June of '97, Garth had found my father living in a state of near starvation even though he lived only about five hundred feet from my oldest brother. He had Alzheimer's disease and could no longer live alone.

When I visited him in the convalescent home, I found him in a small sitting room. He was tied to a chair in a row of elderly people across from another row of the same. I knew none of these people would leave there alive. When we first saw me, his face lit up and I think for a second he thought I was my Mom. We stayed for a while walking with him, taking him outside, making conversation. By the time we were leaving it was supper time. We took him back to the sitting room. Just as we were approaching the sitting room, a nurse came towards my father and did a little dance step, kidding with him. He smiled and for an instant he looked just like Bree. His expression was like Bree S when I danced with her. It was a struggle to keep back my tears. How could I leave him there, drugged to keep him calm... and with strangers? I hugged him and said that I loved him. That was the last time we spoke.

It was a three hour ride home and I cried all the way. I wanted to bring my father home with me, to put him in the back seat with Bree. I wanted him to be with us. I had fought against the idea of placing Bree in an institution for eighteen years and I hated to have him in one, yet my hands were tied. I lived in another country where there was no general social health care system. I was living on welfare and caring for Bree full time. My mind went through all the pros and cons of having him with us. So he was in diapers... so what, just a bigger Bree. My father was now this beautiful little boy who needed warm care. Gone was the lame ego that made him feel he had to be the strongest, the best. Gone were the wise cracks that cut through my heart. The visit was the best memory I have of my father. This person would have been easy to love. This person would have been incapable of seeking ways to control, to manipulate my mother.

I spent days thinking about how it be possible to have Dad live with is. No one encouraged me which I guess was normal because no one had encouraged me with Bree. I had heard that he could be violent if he was not on his medicine and that he might choke to death. In response, I said that he could sit on the couch watching Bree as we went through our daily routine. At least he would be part of a family. The bottom line was that it was impractical, unrealistic. Our society does not support keeping our loved ones at home, reasoning that it is too much responsibility, too time taking, too demanding. I just watched a video recently called *Down On The Far*, which was an excellent example of a family taking on the responsibility. The niece asked her uncle, who was caring for his wife, "Aren't there homes for people like her?"

He replied, "She is home."

My father died about one month after that visit. I was once again coming from Montreal and had stopped in for a visit. When I walked into his room, I knew he was dying, that it was just a matter of days. A nurse told me that he had a cold and would be put on antibiotics as soon as they arrived. This was on Monday. The died on Friday morning.

It had been impossible for me to stay with him for I had no one to care for Bree. Garth and my brother Richard were with him for the last four days. It was difficult for them and I shall always appreciate the fact that they were at his side, so he was not alone. I feel sure that he and my mother now lend me support from the spiritual realm.

We went to stay with my brother Garth before the funeral. He told us he had discovered that my brother Ronnie had been getting my dad to write him monthly check to the tune of at least $12,000 a year. My brother had been taking advantage of my father for a long while, something I found very difficult to understand. Ronnie had always been afraid of getting old. Once he asked my sister Cheryl, "Why is it that Wendy is the only one in the family who never ages?" I have often thought it strange that my two oldest brothers had the same parents as the rest of the family because their outlook on life is so different.

And now back to my financial problems. My life was never going to change as long as Bree lived, yet my support systems were shutting down as she aged. With our welfare rug being pulled out from under us in less than a year, I had to find some way to earn some money.

The Kushi Institute in the Berkshires is the teaching center for macrobiotics on the east coast. There was a three-level training program that might make it possible for me to earn some money while still caring for Bree. The only option that I could see was to get some training in the lifestyle we were living. I had no idea how this would work, where the money would be coming from. I decided to look into the possibility of getting qualified to be a Macrobiotic teacher and counselor. I telephoned the Kushi Institute and asked for information and whether they offered any form of scholarships. Then I started talking with people in general about finding ways to finance this venture. I knew that even if I didn't end up teaching, what I learned would help me improve Bree's care.

The first breakthrough came when the Institute offered me a scholarship of $1000 per level and they agreed to let Bree be with me during my courses. The staff had seen us at their summer sessions for one week over the past thirteen years. I had worked as a volunteer in their bookstore and attended all the events with Bree. They knew from these experiences that Bree would not disturb the classes in any way. I spent days calling one organization after another trying to find the financial support for the $6000 I would need to complete all three levels. I asked friends for suggestions about where to ask. The three levels were lined up back to back from April 16th through the end of July one week off between each level. I received enough donations to get me through the first level and I signed up for that. I figured I would take the first step, hoping to raise more money before I needed it to continue.

If I became qualified to teach Macrobiotics, it would be the answer to my prayers. I knew there was barely a year before our financial woes would increase and I continued the telephone calls and filled out applications to various organizations. I was put on the first list of tentative students for levels two and three even though the money hadn't been raised yet. I had to do this because the number of available spaces was limited. The classes were for a maximum of twenty-three students. I figured it would work out if God meant it to be.

A week before starting Level 1, we drove to the Berkshires with my housemate/partner, Peter, to see the layout – the sleeping quarters – and to find out what I would need to take for Bree. The Kushi Institute was three hours from my home. I would be making this trip every weekend for the next four months, more or less.

As the starting date got closer, I began having nosebleeds. I had one on our first visit that was hard to stop. We were down in the basement in an area for students to relax. There was a place to watch television and a small kitchen where I would be able to heat up Bree's meals. I figure the nosebleeds were a cry for love and an emotional reaction to the stress I had been undergoing just to get qualified. How would I get through the classes and the studying and still care for Bree? At home we had our established routine. What if Bree got sick? Was I insane to even attempt this? What if I kept having nosebleeds? I was just straight out scared. The only comforting thought was that I had been practicing this way of life for fourteen years. Surely that should make levels one and two familiar and fairly easy. Most of the teachers I knew from the lectures they had given at the summer conference. I could always back out, but at least I had to try.

Peter drove down with us the following weekend as it took two cars to transport all the stuff to make our room as familiar as possible for Bree. There were her futon, magnetic bed pad, sheets, towels, diapers, clothes for all types of weather, favorite toys, her carriage, and books. I knew from experience that the more organized I was and the faster I set up a routine for Bree, the better chance I had of making it through the course.

I was excited about being at the Kushi Institute and I wanted to complete the course, yet I wondered whether I had gotten in way over my head. The macrobiotic lifestyle had added years to Bree's life. It was quite literally the foundation of our lives. The idea of being able to teach others about it held great appeal and I felt people would listen more intently to someone with initials after her name. A dream of mine was to teach parents of brain-injured children about this lifestyle.

It was refreshing to be around people who lived the same way I did. It made me feel more normal. The first month was really tough but thank heaven the subject matter was familiar. I had given up coffee, maple sugar, and all baked goods as they all aided nosebleeds, especially the combination of coffee and maple syrup. So I no longer had the nosebleeds but during the first month I had headaches and a runny nose. I didn't dare blow my nose for fear of starting it bleeding. It felt as if I was just barely hanging in there from class to class. The schedule was hard as we had a lot to learn in one month. I was not used to being a student. On many days school began at 9:30 in the morning and lasted to 9:30 at night. During breaks when classmates were having a snack or getting acquainted, I was carrying Bree back to our room for a diaper change. At lunch time I had two to feed and then clean up after. There were two or three night classes. Before them I had to get Bree ready for bed and make sire there was some music playing for her.

Our room for the first two months was on the first floor next to the dining hall. This seemed ideal but it turned out to be a nightmare. Our bedroom was above the television area where staff and students partied every night. In the early morning we would be awakened by staff in the kitchen which was next to the dining hall. The only thing that saved me was getting home on weekends and trying to catch up on sleep there. On these weekends there was the laundry to be done and the preparation of Bree's food to take back. I was so tired and nervous that it was a struggle to get through each day. Thinking about finishing the three levels was more than I could handle. Yet I believed if I gave up then I would never get back to accomplish my aims.

The teachers were very understanding when I had to leave class to attend to Bree and she was wonderful. As long as she was fed and changed she was happy leaning against me in class, having so many new people to draw into her circle of what I called "Breeness". She has a way of drawing people in and then working on them spiritually. Most people have no idea of the old powerful soul they have just come into contact with. For Bree it was an ongoing party.

At the end of the first week, Bree came down with a twenty-four hour cold, but I really think it was her way of adjusting to the new lifestyle. She was back to normal on Monday. I was concerned because I knew that continuing depended on her health and well-being. I have learned that what is good for Bree turns out to be good for me. If the situation was not good for Bree, it would be impossible for me to continue.

We made it through the first month and then had a weeks off before the next level. On the last day there was a graduation party. Some students would not be continuing at this time. There were about seven of us who planned to do all the levels back to back. I believe we were the first ones to do this. One thing that made this possible for me was a foundation in New Hampshire called High Hopes which grants a wish for a child between the ages of thirteen and eighteen who has a life-threatening illness. Bree was accepted because she was living long past the five years she had been given at birth. All the information I learned would improve and refine the quality of her life. When I received the telephone call from High Hopes telling me the remaining cost would be paid for, I knew it was the answer to my prayers. Before my prayers had been questions: "Should I try to do this?", "Will it work out doing it back-to-back?", "Will I be able to do it with Bree?" Receiving the money convinced me that everything would work out. God wanted me to finish the course. This kept me going. When doubts would pop into my mind, I would remind myself that the money had appeared when I needed it. I had asked the foundation for enough money for one more level, but they basically paid for two.

When I got home for the first break, I was sick for three days with chills and fever. I think I was just worn out, but I knew I could take time to rest up because I was safe at home.

My favorite class was the Shiatsu which was totally new to me. I was amazed that I had been practicing the macrobiotic lifestyle for fourteen years and yet had not realized how important a part of Shiatsu was. I knew immediately that this was a practice I wanted in my life. Shiatsu is a form of oriental massage that uses both feet and hands. When

I am giving a treatment, I can tell the body condition of the person I am massaging. Aches and pains, skin color, and flexibility are some of the tools by which I can know a person's conditions and then can suggest better food choices. It became obvious to me how true the saying is, "You are what you eat." Shiatsu was the missing link for me in my macrobiotic practice.

The Kushi Institute had a new program whereby if I completed the three levels of training and then submitted proof of one hundred hours of giving Shiatsu treatments, I could become a member of the American Oriental Bodywork Therapy Association (A. O. B. T. A.). This was at the Kushi Institute at the right time because I hoped to be certified. God was watching over me!

Bree loved the Shiatsu classes as she got to be one the floor with the rest of us. She enjoyed watching us work with one another but especially enjoyed the beginning when we did swinging arm movements. She would sing... making her ah-ah and el-el sounds. Towards the end of the second level, Bree and I were in our Shiatsu class doing our warming up exercises and she started "signing" and some class members answered her sounds. Bree was delighted. I told the class that for two months she had been wanting them to join her. I was thrilled because they were starting to understand her instead of fearing her. Bree had been accepted as a member of the class.

Shiatsu is the healing art that comes to us from Japan. The form I was learning was called Barefoot Shiatsu because half the treatment was given by the hands, arms, and fingers and the other half by the soles of their feet. The receiver wears loose cotton clothing. Having someone work on your body is very personal and I really like this form of massage. I knew that I myself felt more comfortable working on someone with clothes on and also was more comfortable being worked on clothed. The more experience I got, the more convinced I was that I was good at this. Perhaps it was from working with Bree so many years that made it come easily to me. I began singing up friends for free massages to complete the one hundred hours, hopefully before Christmas. No on had accomplished this at the Institute and I wanted to be the first. My treatments took close to two hours. Our teachers told us to try and complete the treatments in one hour, but I didn't want it to be a question of trying to beat the clock, but rather a rejuvenating experience. Before I began a treatment, I explained that the way to understand what was happening was to imaging twelve major rivers that flow through the body feeding one's organs with energy. These rivers get blocked as a result of stress. Then I say to imagine me as the person who cleans out the rivers so water (energy) can flow again. As the Shiatsu practitioner, I dig out the sand and rocks that have accumulated.

When I had my first treatment, I felt so good that everything was flowing again. I experienced a wonderful sense of well-being and afterward I slept so peacefully that I knew it was very different from a regular massage. The body seems to work along with the massage, making it feel better than just a relaxing experience. My Ki (energy in Japanese) was flowing throughout my body, giving me a better understanding of where my body's strengths and weaknesses were. I was convinced that Shiatsu would add a great deal to any future work I did in Macrobiotics. Learning his method of massage was, I believe, the most important part of my schooling. It would give me a chance to earn money for our support.

All my classes were great and I was dealing well with everything except getting a good night's sleep. Towards the end of the second level, I was extremely tired because of lack of sleep. Sometimes I would wake up in the morning to ask the kitchen staff to please shut the doors between the kitchen and the hall. In the middle of some nights I would go down to the basement to ask the young people to please be more quiet as I could hear everything in my bed just above them. I could understand about being twenty-two and not needed much sleep, but I was getting pretty ragged. I found myself crying at the drop of a hat. There was no way I could go through the next level unless I could change my room. Two classmates were planning on buying a mobile home which would free their room, a large one upstairs with a half bath. It was questionable whether I could get that room because all my classmates were coming back and there would be new students for level one. The Institute was over-booked for the month of July and some were having to sleep in tents. I went to the main office and explained the situation. It was obvious that I was stressed out and feeling overwhelmed as I was in tears. Miria, the woman who assigned rooms, said she would so something for me, but she could not promise me the room with the half bath.

It surprises me now that I didn't ask for a different room after two weeks. I think the reasons were that I didn't like rocking the boat and I was so happy that Bree and I had been accepted into the program that I didn't want to complain. I don't believe I could have continued on if I had not gone home every weekend.

Sometimes when I slip out of a class for a cup of tea, I would return to find Bree surrounded by her new friends. One day there was one Japanese friend on each side of her and one at her feet. They were singing to her and Hiro, who was sitting on her right, was blocking her face so I could not see how much fun they were having. It was so sweet the way there were playing games. It was as if they were letting me know I did not have to be there. One nice thing about the Kushi Institute is that people come to it from all over the world. Hiro was becoming an especially good friend and one day I mentioned that if she ever wanted to improve her English, she was more than welcome to spend some time with us in New Hampshire.

On the last day of the second level, I was standing in line for breakfast when Hiro came over and asked if my offer was still open. She would be flying back to Japan in about a week and a half and had nowhere else to stay. Since Bree and I would be coming back to the Institute in a week, Hiro could come back with us and then get a ride from there to Boston. It was settled and Hiro spent a week with us. What a joy that was… the best house guest ever! Hiro and Bree have the same numbers (2-1-9) in a form of astrology called Nine Star Ki. In some ways they were so similar that it was like having a second daughter for a week. Bree was eighteen and Hiro was twenty-seven. Firo had the same energy level as Bree. We went for long walks and I introduced her to all Bree's and my favorite places. One of these was Morgan Hill Bookstore. I was surprised to learn that Connie, one of the store owners, had lived in Japan many years before and was able to say a few welcoming words to Hiro. I wanted Hiro to feel safe and comfortable. I remembered being in Europe when I was in my twenties and what a difference it made when I got to know some local people. Bree and I had a friend to share for a week. This was new for me because usually I was the only one in the area living the macrobiotic lifestyle. For Hiro, coming to my home was a transition place. We ate with chopsticks, slept on futons, ate Japanese style foods even though we were in North America.

The week passed all too quickly and we were on our way back to Kushi. I gave a letter to Hiro to give to the Consulate in Japan when she asked to return to visit us. I knew we could help her learn English as there would be no Japanese friends around like the ones she had at the Institute. I showed her the room she would have. She said it was too big for her. I said, "No Hiro, it is just right for you." She hoped to come back in a couple of months. Meanwhile I'd be taking my final level.

Bree and I did get the room with a half bath. What a wonderful difference that room made. There were a lot of tests and this should have been the hardest level, but for me it was easier than the first one. Bree loved it all. There was always someone who wanted to sit with her, to comb her hair, and even carry her up the stairs for me. Bree was having the time of her life.

Being at the Kushi Institute meant that we were all interested in holistic health and we shared information with each other. I shared my Caroline Myss tapes and videos and my classmates loaned me their tapes and videos. One new friend, Jane Weber, loaned me a book about using a rebounder, saying it could be very good for Bree. A rebounder had is a small round trampoline. The book had a section about how successful using a rebounder had been with handicapped people. There were pictures of people in wheelchairs who sat on them or just had their feet on one and someone else who did the jumping on the rebounder, but the handicapped person felt good results. I was told about children who had them in their classrooms and had good results after a year of daily use. They could walk and talk better and there were other improvements. I learned that using the rebounder increases the pull of gravity on our bodies and this gravitational force improves the condition and tone of body cells and strengthens them.

I knew this could be very helpful for Bree. This would keep her lymph system clean which is so important to maintaining good health. Bree could sit cross-legged between my legs and I could do the work. Bree had always loved my dancing with her, but now she was too heavy for me to hold and dance around the room. The rebounder exercise would be a great addition to our daily routine. It would not only be good for her health, but it would be fun. The benefits would be improved coordination and balance, increased stamina and endurance, and, hopefully, improve intelligence.

Jane was kind and loaned me her rebounder while were were at the Institute. We made an agreement that if she and her friends wanted to use it, they could do so in my room. On weekends, of course, they had it exclusively. This worked out very well. We started doing a five minute session between classes and during lunch and supper breaks. Bree loved it.

My concern had been that she was not getting enough exercise, sitting on the couch next to me during classes. There were couches in the library and chapel which were our main lecture areas. The building had been a hunting lodge and then was a Franciscan Monastery. The building where we slept, ate, and had most of our classes was where the monks slept, ate, studied, and prayed. At 6:30 a.m. we had a mindful meditation gathering which gave me a chance to get centered for the day. Then came the "Do-in" class at 7. This is a self-managed technique. I loved this class because it was help in the chapel. Usually I had to slip out of this class to get Bree up, dressed, and fed. It felt just right for Bree and me to be in a place that was a monastery, learning about a traditional way of life. How fortunate I was to be able to get qualification in the macrobiotic system when it had been what kept Bree alive, drug-free, and healthy.

A water problem developed… no water! The Institute had to resort to bottled water. It was the hottest time of the year and the classes were over-booked. What a time to be out of water! I help on for a day and then went to the general manager and told him I would have to take Bree home until I could be assured of having safe water. Heeping her clean and comfortable without running water was impossible. (Had I come this far only to have to give up?) I said I didn't want to problem to affect my final testing. He said that would not be a problem, so I went home for a couple of days. Then even when we returned, we had to use bottled water for drinking and brushing our teeth for the remainder of our stay. This time at the Institute had shown how lonely it had been for me all these years leading this lifestyle alone. It is always special sharing an intense experience. For a short period of time I felt like a member of a large family. I was so grateful to the staff for allowing me to have Bree there.

During that last week there were many tests, oral and written. I always worried about taking tests. The one problem I ran into was on the night og the written exam. It was hot and mosquitoes had gotten into the room. Bree was tired and I had to try to keep the mosquitoes off her. Finally I gave up the struggle. I wrote on my paper that I had to put Bre to bed and would finish the test some other time.

The next morning the manager told me that if I was serious about getting my Shiatsu certification, I would have to redo that test. I asked when and said I would be available the next day. The Shiatsu teacher saw me in the parking lot and I explained the situation to him. He understood and yet I got the impression that men do not realize how difficult it is for a mother to concentrate when her child is not comfortable. The next day I took the test and smiled when I saw that the teacher had changed the questions. That did not matter for at the end of the exam I knew I had aced it. All that remained was my personal review with the teachers.

The main teacher, the general manager, and Aveline Kushi were at this review. I took only half an hour, yet it was the most positive evaluation I've ever had. When my cooking teacher, Myumi, said that my cooking tasted as if Mrs. Kushi herself had prepared the dishes, it took me quite a while to absorb this. I considered this the highest compliment I could have received. Mrs. Kushi turned my way and bowed her head, expressing a sound of praise – ahhhh! Another teacher, Charles Millman, told me that I have a quick mind and that I could have absorbed twice as much information. My Shiatsu teacher said I was the best student… and it went on and on... most serious; best; good, quick answers. Never had I had such praise, never had I been the best student. During that half hour it seemed as if God said, "I am proud of you, Wendy." Finally, after all the years of work with Bree when I had tried to do my best, I received confirmation from people I respected for their knowledge.

How well I had done really came through when I talked with Ed Esko, the man in charge of signing up people for the Macrobiotic Educators Association exam. This was a week-long test that would put me at the highest level I could reach in Macrobiotics. When I asked what books I needed to read in preparation for the exam, he said I was ready without more reading. Then the man who sets up the M. E. A testing told me that I was the valedictorian of the class. This a long way from the insecure kid who barely scraped through high school. I could succeed in doing what what I loved. This was an eye opener for me. I had spent years working alone with Bree, never getting praise for my work and having to fight for every break-through. I knew it would take me awhile to absorb the significance of this. I also knew that at some point in the future I would be teaching Macrobiotics along with being a Shiatsu practitioner, but I still wasn't sure how this could be combined with the full time care of Bree. Yet, I had made it through all three levels with her at my side. I must have had angelic help!

My next step was to complete my three hundred hours of Shiatsu in order to be certified to teach. I had already completed some and I had friends signed up for treatments beginning in August. My goal was to finish before Christmas. I had no idea how this would change our financial outlook by the time April second (Bree's birthday) rolled around, but this is what I could do in the meantime. I figured that if I put my best food forward, somehow things would work out.

I was now qualified in Macrobiotic career training, had all the requirements for membership in the American Oriental Bodywork Therapy Association, and qualified to practice Reiki, a form of laying on of hands in healing. My unfinished projects were to finish this book, write a cookbook for brain-injured, and a storybook for children. The problem with these projects was that none would give me badly needed income immediately. My training so far was a wonderful help in working with Bree. Now to use it to earn money. I hoped somehow God would make things work out for us.

Between caring for Bree and keeping myself on an even keel, the days flew by. As April approached I became more and more nervous and I began having dizzy spells which I blamed on being stretched out. I was calling all my case workers at welfare, social security, and Community Bridges asking for guidance… in tears… yet I was getting nowhere. The common response I received indicated that Bree and I had fallen through the cracks. I kept asking the different organizations what happens to a single mom at home with a child who needs full time care. Were they put out on the street because that child had turned nineteen? My situation did not change because of Bree's birthday. She would receive welfare as an independent person, but I would no longer get welfare and would not have health care coverage. Not only was Bree getting older, but so was I. Chances were that I would need more health care benefits in the future. The state was willing to pay $125,000 a year to put Bree in an institution but would not support a single parent at home, the one who could provide the best and healthiest care. When I asked what others in a similar position did, the only feedback I received indicated that they either were better off financially or that they had gone the institutional route. It seemed hopeless to me and my dizziness increased. Was there something seriously wrong with me? Did I have a threatening disease? Such thoughts made me panic. If I died, who would care for Bree? Even God seemed far away. It felt like the "dark night of the soul"! My needs did not seem to matter.

The most confusing thing for me was the fact that I was more than willing to care for my daughter on a day to day basis, yet our society does not support care giving. When the dizziness started, I got out my old faithful book, *Heal Your Life*. In the center of the book is a list of diseases with the probably negative thoughts that help make them manifest, along with positive alternatives. It was right there. Dizziness is scattered thinking. My inability to see a way out of my situation "scattered my thinking". The positive affirmation for elevating dizziness is to say, "I am deeply centered and peaceful. It is safe for me to be alive and joyous." This was the opposite of what I had been feeling. Until I could find a way to survive financially, feeling secure and peaceful was out of the question.

In March the telephone rang. It was a woman named Melissa from an agency who asked me what kind of services would help me. The poor woman got an earful of frustration and tears from me. Once again I could get nursing care for Bree, medicines, and equipment… all the things I had worked for twenty years not to need. I told her I needed money to pay our monthly upkeep. I felt I was wasting my time. Neither one of us knew how the information about me ended up on her desk, but it turned out fortuitous. After listing all the possibly services for agency could provide, I asked her to please go through them again. When she said I could have a housekeeper to clean my house, I said I'd better look into that. My thought was that I might make good use of the hour or two the house was being cleaned. It didn't seem like much, but I was ready to grab at straws. We completed all the necessary forms and had a good mom-to-mom talk. She has a little girl and I could see her frustration when she saw that I was not looking for someone else to do my work but just needed financial help. As she left, Melissa said that she could not promise anything but that she would show her boss the newspaper article about Bree. I felt her visit had been a waste of time. She was a nice person, but I had spent the morning answering question to apply for a housekeeper, the least of my needs at that time.

It felt like I was going nowhere fast. I kept sharing my story, looking for possible opportunities but coming up with services I didn't really need. If I did get help in housekeeping, It could free up my time for doing something or other… God only knew that! I had done all I could to prepare for the transition when Bree's birthday came. I was keeping her healthy and managing to keep my sanity.

About a week and a half later, Melissa called. She said she had great news for me. She had talked with her boss and he had given his approval to put me in a program that was being phased out called HCBC. This program would pay me a minimum wage to stay home and care for

Bree which was just what I had been requesting. My first comment was "This seems too good to be true!" Then I asked what was meant by "being phased out." Did it mean I would be put on a program and then be cut off later?

"No, my boss has made an exception for you," she said, "No one new is being put on this program."

Bree and I had just slipped in. Melissa's boss said that help for me had been a long time coming and I deserved a break. To facilitate this program, I would have to go through another interview, fill out forms, and then be hired by the Concord Regional Visiting Nurses Association and meet all their standard procedures. Within a month I could be receiving a weekly salary for doing what I do best: care for my own child. It still would be the least expensive deal around as I would be making less than half of what a stranger would, but for me it was a breakthrough. God had come through again at the eleventh hour! I told Melissa that until all the "i's" were dotted and I received my first paycheck, I was not going to let myself get too excited. I wanted this to work out so much that I was afraid something could go wrong. I did tell her how much I appreciated what she had done for us, an angel in disguise. I wondered about the parents of other brain-injured children because this was being phased out. Maybe I would have to be the one to help bring about changes for the moms who would follow me.

Chapter 19

Bree has had her twentieth birthday... how wonderful! To think that when she was born she was given the prognosis of five years at most. I don't know how to put into words how grateful I am. At her birth, I asked God, "What did I do wrong to be given a brain-injured child?" Now after twenty years my question is, "What did I do right to be granted the privilege to be Bree's caregiver and mom?" The first eight to ten years of her life I was pretty much in a state of panic, feeling as if I was racing against the clock just to keep Bree alive. The next ten years were spent maintaining the care giving and trying to get a firm emotional footing. Now we have arrived at the plateau of just being! Sometimes it seems as if Bree was just waiting for me to grow enough to be able to appreciate her presence in my life.

Care giving is a daily routine. What for others may seem monotonous effort... like feeding, changing diapers, and dressing has become what I do day after day, but our life together, for the most part, is pure joy. Our days are simple, structured, and yet so good. Now that my financial worries have lessened considerably and now that I have help from the education system with teaching aids, Bree and I are able to thoroughly enjoy our togetherness. At the moment I am writing this, I can hear her in the Shiatsu room with her school aid Jane King. Bree is making all the happy sounds sounds, "aaah, aaah-ei, ee," that tell me she is having a good time. When matters are not progressing so well, Bree will ask for my attention by giving a quick sniff.

So what makes up our days? First thing is the waking up process, a slow but pleasurable one for Bree who likes to do a lot of stretching. Usually by then I have been up reading and writing in my journal for an hour or two and it's nice to slip into Bree's bed and snuggle for five or ten minutes before opening the drapes and deciding on an outfit for the day. Then I feed her breakfast. At the present time our mornings are pretty much open except for Tuesdays and Fridays when her physiotherapist, Mary Winslow, comes for an hour and Wednesdays when Linda Lucas comes at eight o'clock for a feeding session. Bree is being taught to feed herself with the aid of a wooden bowl and special long-handled spoon. I had the bowl made especially for her with a lip on the sides as I did not want her to use plastic. Linda helps during these sessions by scooping the food onto the spoon, then Bree does the rest. There are two other times during the weeks that Bree has feeding sessions. They are on Monday and Thursday for Supper. Joni Horning, Bree's school aid, does the other feedings. Bree has a school aid ten hours a weeks. Jane King works six hours and Joni the other four.

What we call Bree's social calendar consists of three hours Monday afternoon with Jane followed by a 4:30 supper with Joni. After lunch on Tuesdays Joni volunteers her time to entertain Bree. She sings songs accompanied by the autoharp or guitar. Bree loves this time and I make myself scarce as this is her time with her special buddy. Joni also spends three hours on Thursday afternoons combining music and reading out loud before she helps Bree eat her supper. She snuggles up to Bree and calls "my hot ticket" in such a loving way that Bree responds by making the happy sounds which are unique to her. It was a very special happening when Joni Horning came into our lives! Along with all this Joni Grey, her chiropractor, comes every two weeks and Robert Bishop, (Dr. B, as we call him), her osteopath, comes twice a week... When Bree is with these friends, I am busy cooking, shopping, or doing errands... like going to the post office, the bank, the pharmacy, the library, or the hardware store.

When we are alone, Bree and I enjoy the trampoline. We have been doing this forty five minutes a day for the last two years. I try to read aloud to Bree for at least an hour each day. We have just finished the second volume of *The Lord of the Rings* and are about to read the third and final volume. We also meditate daily for forty-five minutes, using the Kabat-Zinn Lying Down method. We had been doing this for years. Bree spends the time pulling my hair, playing with her mirror toy, or taking a little snooze. When the tape gets to the "now you are wide awake" part, she is ready with a big stretch. There are still moments when panic sets in if Bree appears out of sorts or ill. I immediately find myself doing a mental checklist of what could be the cause. Fortunately problems of this sort are infrequent.

In warm weather we usually walk four miles a day. Fresh air and sunshine are very good for Bree and pushing over a hundred pounds of Bree and the stroller keeps me fit. A good walk is an excellent way to work out emotional frustrations. I am hoping to get a better stroller, one with a hood and leaf cover to keep out the rain and a leg warmer for colder weather. This new stroller could double our walking time. If I am fortunate, the stroller will be approved by medicaid and another foundation will pay for the accessories, as medicaid does not approve anything for health and well being but only for what they call a medical necessity which has to be approved by a doctor. The stroller does not come with any type of storage area, such as a wheelchair pack, which would be convenient for a hat, gloves, or library books. This would only be approved if Bree needed an oxygen bottle or drugs. As per usual, there is so much red tape and delay after delay before any request is finalized that it can be very frustrating. How wonderful it would be if I were in the position of just going out and buying the stroller myself! To be financially independent is something I hope for our future… a dream?

During our walks I have never seen a brain-injured child being walked even though I know there are many brain-injured children and adults. My experience has shown me that no one is out walking with any of them just for the pure pleasure of being outside. I also know that many people in town like to see us walking because I have been told so. "I saw you yesterday," and "I missed seeing you," are the comments I often receive.

One important aspect I have had to face is what if I should die? What would happen about Bree's care? A will of life insurance seemed essential. Then the question about how I would be able to face Bree's death was another stickler. How difficult the idea of that happening was to face and yet I felt convinced I should be prepared in order not to make wrong decisions that I would regret. The life of a parent of a brain-injured child is far different from that of other parents in that we want our children to die before we do. For other parents it is a tragedy to have a child die first, but for us, the parents who strive constantly to keep our hurt children alive and safe, the worst thing would be to have them outlive us, because we cannot be sure anyone else would give them the loving care we do. We pray for our children to live as long as possible and at the same time we pray that they will die peacefully in their sleep when that time comes. Who else would devote twenty-four hours a day, every day... year after year?

Difficult questions with no easy answers! In the book *Something More – Excavating Your Authentic Self,* Sarah Ban Breathnach wrote about a family whose little daughter Alison died because of an accident with an airbag. They had a vigil instead of a conventional funeral. I knew when I read this that I would have to find out more. I remember as a child walking past the living room door and seeing my grandfather Gilker laid in his coffin. Ever since the whole idea of death has bothered me and thinking about Bree's death seemed too much for me to handle. Ten years ago I could not visualize life without Bree. Now I can because I know there is so much I can do working with parents of brain-injured children to help make their lives easier and, hopefully, more rewarding. This could be a life's work, making good use of all I have learned from caring for Bree all these years. There are so many more books to read... so much more to discover.

It was difficult, but I made myself get in touch with the organization Crossings: Caring for Our Own at Death. I ordered their resource guide because I want to regret. After my mom's death there were so many things I wished I had done differently, like crawling into bed with her at the hospital and holding her when she died. I also wished I had not gone to see her at the funeral home which made made my last memory of her that of someone who did not resemble her at all. Another regret... there was no family participation at her funeral. Instead, a stranger talked about someone he did not know. Never again will I let a scary situation intimidate me with withdrawal and regrets.

When the information came from Crossings, it sat on my desk for weeks while I tried to get brave enough to sit down and read through it. I know now that when the time comes, there is a guide in my file drawer for me to follow.

In highschool I read the poem "The Road Less Traveled" by Robert Frost which I loved instantly. At that time I did not know why it impressed me so much, just that I hoped I could live my own life that way. The final lines of the poem are:

Two Roads diverged in a wood, and I took the one less traveled by. And that made all the difference.

I feel that I have taken the road less traveled by, caring for Bree at home for these last twenty years when everyone I know would have supported me in committing her to an institution. My life is so much better because I did not opt out by using the excuse that I would not be able to handle it. What I have gained is having a happy and well behaved person, my pride and joy. Part of the explanation for this is that Bree, due to our macrobiotic lifestyle, is free of all medications and their side effects. She does not eat sugar or foods with any additive or chemicals of any kind. I read about a study that was done at the Tidewater Detention Center in Chesapeake, Virginia where they gave juvenile offenders a new diet. Infractions dropped a startling forty-five percent just by the removal of sugar.

Lately there had been a great deal of research done in the field of allergens, some with surprising results. A single allergen can cause as many as fifteen or more reactions from mood swings, itchy and runny noses and eyes, canker sores, migraine headaches, to epileptic seizures. Brain-injured children are prone to getting these seizures. The most frequent allergens responsible for convulsive reactions are found in foods. The most common of these are milk, eggs, wheat, chocolate, beef, pork, veal, and cheese. A report in the December , 1951 edition of "Modern Medicine" by Susan C. Dees, M.D. and Hans Lowenbach, M.D.

stated that in a study of thirty-seven children who had either grand mal or petit mal seizures, all allergic symptoms and all seizures were controlled when the foods to which they were allergic to were eliminated. Reading about this confirmed what I had experienced with Bree. I have never had a doctor tell me anything about this. What surprises me even more is that I have never had a doctor show any interest when I shared my experience with Bree… that by eliminating all dairy products, sugar, animal foods, strawberries, and wheat products, her grand mal seizures stopped.

There is a book by Gary Null with Dr. Martin Feldman, *Good Food, Good Mood*, which shows how the foods we eat can be linked to ailments seldom associated with allergies. In Macrobiotics we saw that if you want your children to stop fighting with each other, then remove sugar from their diet. My experience has shown me that a brain-injured child on a grain, plant-based diet with no sugar or animal foods is a very happy, healthy person.

Every May in New Hampshire there is a conference for the parents of brain-injured children to inform them about different options for their children. Two years ago I applied to present information on food choices and what I experienced with a grain-based diet and to date they have shown no interest. I have yet to understand why people will opt to take medication with side effects and refuse to take the time to change their choices… why people believe in drugs as a solution instead of the healing ability of God-given foods.

Bree's birthday party when she turned twenty was wonderful. All the years when I had tried to have conventional parties because I thought it was expected are behind me. A party perfect for Bree is what matters. Joni and Chick Horning asked to come over and sing to her. Then I invited Jane King to come with her drum and her husband with his guitar and a party was soon forming. I prepared lots of good macrobiotic food and asked our neighbor Marti to join us, as she used to "sit" Bree, and the party was on.

Bree had a great time because she was with people who loved her. She had her own private concert for two hours with the people who work with her the most. I taped an hour of the singing to send to her grandmother Gilker, so she could hear Bree's affirming sounds of joys and happiness during the entertainment. Bree was so happy that when she went to bed, it took her a long time to to to sleep. After prayers she made happy sounds of contentment for at least half an hour. It was not birthday cake and candles or presents she wanted. It was being with people who loved her and accepted her for the hot ticket she really is.

Why do so many people feel threatened by brain-injured children? Love is what Bree is all about. She giggles when she creeps out of the bathroom after her bath and make happy sounds as I get her to creep over to the futon couch and get her to climb up for reading time. Sometimes she things the way I chew my food is hilarious. When she sits between my legs on the trampoline and looks up at me with her dear face, her expression says, "Okay. You are here, Mom." and my heart melts. When I get out her jacket and she knows that mom is taking her somewhere, and it does not matter where, she excitedly heads for the jacket. This is enchantment. Bree reminds me to have fun. What a privilege it is to share her life.

In Morris West's book, *The Clowns of God*, he has his character Jean Marie hold a Downs Syndrome child in his arms as he talks to the Assembly:

> "I do not know what you are thinking. You need a sign. What better one could I give than to make this little one whole and new? I could do it; but I will not. I am the Lord and not a conjuror. I gave this mite a gift I denied to all you… eternal innocence. To you she looks imperfect, but to me she is flawless, like the bud that dies unopened or the fledgling that falls from the the nest to be devoured by the ants. She will never offend me, as all of you have done. She will never pervert or destroy the works of my father's hands. She is necessary to you. She will evoke the kindness that will keep you human. Her infirmity will prompt you to gratitude for your own good fortune… More! She will remind you everyday that I am who I am, that my ways are not yours, and that the smallest dust mote whirled in darkest space does not fall

out of my hand… I have chosen you. You have not chosen me. This little one is your sign. Treasure her!"

Thank God that I have Bree, my innocent charmer, to treasure. And what a blessing it is to realize that within every little ugly duckling lies potential for being transformed into a beautiful swan!

Epilogue

May 8, 2016

Bree is now 36 years old. She is still holding her own creeping around the house, making her happy sounds and knowing what she wants and letting me know about it. She is healthy considering the involvement of her deletion, not even having a cold in several years.

I have maintained the foundations of what was set up during the 20 years. We still practice a macrobiotic lifestyle and Bree is still creeping around the house every day. The plant based diet and what we learned from the Institutes for the Achievement of Human Potential have been and continue to be vital in raising Bree. Of course, there have been changes. As my knowledge grows I tweak things here and there. I have added green smoothies and more raw foods to our diet and I do the parts of the stimulation program that I can manage. Bree only sees a doctor once a year for her annual checkup which is required by our local agency.

I am a single mom and have been most of this journey with Bree. It has been hard financially more than anything else, along with the stress and anxiety that comes with that. Yes, Bree means full, 24/7 care and that level of care is very demanding, yet Bree is a joy. She is just this pure, beautiful soul who never has a negative thought depending on me to keep her safe healthy.

I have said many times that – Bree is not the problem – the system we live in is the problem. Yes, there has been a great deal of stress whenever BRee is feeling off or coming down with something. A large part of that stress comes from knowing that I have to figure out how to help her myself because if I take her to a doctor they will prescribe a drug of some kind that would devastate her in some way. I will never forget the time the doctor gave her seizure medication (that was too strong for her) and he put Bree into respiratory distress.

Just this morning, Bree woke up feeling off, cranky, looking a bit green and sweating. The old feeling of fear and helplessness still pop up, wondering what is this about. Then I go back to my basics – aspirin suppositories and Kuzu drink. I make up the Kuzu drink and within ½ hour, Bree is making her happy sounds. I still absolutely hate it when Bree is not feeling her best. It is the feeling of helplessness; will I be able to handle this, will I make the right decision, what if she dies and hating that she is in pain? She cannot tell me what it is and is relying on me to make the best decision.

Even, with this sort of stress with Bree, it is small compared with fighting for services and financial support. The bottom line of why that is in our society is because people like my daughter are just not valued in this society. Our society looks upon them as a burden, Our society values people who are young, sing, dance, or act generally. One has to have a job. There is not value in the dignity of caring for a disabled person. What I have learned during the almost 40 years of raising Bree is priceless. It is an experience like no other. And the interesting thing is that no one wants to be me.

During this time, I have fed, dressed, done her hair, brushed her teeth, cut toenails and fingernails, bathed, cooked for, creeped with, read to, massaged, walked, fed, nursed through sickness, and changed thousands of diapers (lots of shit). And loved my girl. Yet that is nothing compared to what Bree has done for me and continues to do for me daily, By caring for Bree, she has saved me. She has made me over. I am a better human being because I have cared for her.

The diet I have chosen to provide for my daughter and myself has and is crucial to our long term health and well-being. It is without a doubt why Bree is still alive and healthy and medication free. The saying "You are what you eat" says it all. What we put into our mouths becomes a powerful biological response modifier, changing the way the body works. The body given the raw materials it needs (plant based, organic foods) is able to heal itself. This is a subject I will cover in my next book based on my 36+ years of preparing and cooking a healing diet for my daughter Bree.

My final book in the Swan/Bree trilogy will be on caregiving. This is the most stressful job on the planet. How does one manage it? How does a parent of a special needs child, not only survive, but manage to continue to care for and support a totally dependant child, their whole life. The financial challenges, health challenges, emotional challenges, and spiritual challenges. This too will be dealt with in future writings.

Our situation is a work in process. It is a one-day-at-a-time process. Each night as I put my daughter to bed, carrying her to bed, I say to myself: *I can do this, I can do this, I can do this.* And then when I changer her diaper at 11 pm, as she sleeps, I feel so blessed to have her safe and sound with me. She is so beautiful. I pray that when it is Bree's time to leave this planet, it will be a quiet passing in her sleep. Until that time, may God continue to make me the parent he wants me to be, show me how to love most patiently, and to be there for her most fully. Amen

This picture shows me comforting Bree when she started crying because her picture was being taken because she doesn't like the flash. The little girl who did not respond to lights, sounds, and touch now does not like the flash of a camera, laughs when I dress her as sometimes it tickles and hears and sees everything that is happening around her. And I am finally in a place to strength with my daughter, confident of the care I provide, free of the medical world with its limited solutions of surgery and medications and able to enjoy being mom and providing a safe, happy and healthy life. Thank you Bree for choosing me.

Wendy and Bree live in New London, New Hampshire

Dear God:

There are no words for the depth of my love for this child of mine – Bree.

I surrender her into your hands. Please dear God, send your angels to protect and surround her always.

May she be protected from the darkness of seizures and sickness, pain and discomfort.

Her body is overtaken with seizures and weakness and I am so scared and overwhelmed.

Please heal her, Lord.

Whatever the words I am supposed to say, whatever the thoughts that would set her free.

I am willing to have them shine into my mind.

Please give me a miracle with Bree.

Please give me hope.

Please give me peace.

Lift me up beyond the regions of my despair and anxiety.

Prepare each cell of Bree's body to be born anew into health and happiness, peace and love, comfort and joy.

For You are the power, not these seizures and disablement.

You are out salvation, not the doctor.

For this is not freedom, and I wish to be free

This is peaceful, and I desire peace.

This is not Your will for us, that I would suffer anxiety and fear or that Bree would feel pain and sickness

I accept Your will for us.

I accept Your healing.

I accept Your love.

I surrender, dear God, my parenthood to You.

Make me the parent You want me to be.

Show me how to love most patiently, to be there for her most fully.

To understand profoundly who she is and what she needs.

May I be a blessing to her now and forever.

Please, dear God, help me.

Amen.

This prayer was inspired by several different prayers I found in *Illuminata* by Marianne Williamson.

THE END

Recommended Books

What To Do About Your Brain-injured Child
by Glenn Doman

How to Teach Your Baby to Be Physically Superb (The Gentle Revolution Series)
by Glenn Doman and Douglas Doman

You the Healer: The World-Famous Silva Method on How to Heal Yourself and Others
by Robert B. Stone and Jóse Silva

The Power of Sound: How to Be Healthy and Productive Using Music and Sound
by Joshua Leeds

The Self Healing Cookbook : A Macrobiotic Primer for Healing Body, Mind and Moods With Whole, Natural Foods
by Kristina Turner

The Complete Macrobiotic Diet: 7 Steps to Feel Fabulous, Look Vibrant, and Think Clearly
by Denny Waxman and Michio Kushi

Mayumi's Kitchen: Macrobiotic Cooking for Body and Soul
by Mayumi Nishimura and Madonna

Don't Drink Your Milk!
by Frank A. Oski

Whitewash: The Disturbing Truth About Cow's Milk and Your Health
by Joseph Keon and John Robbins

Alkalize or Die: Superior Health Through Proper Alkaline-Acid Balance
by Theodore A. Baroody

Resources

The Institutes for the Achievement of Human Potential

Address:
8801 Stenton Avenue
Wyndmoor, PA 19038, USA
Contact Information:
Telephone: (215) 233-2050
Fax: 215-233-9312
Email: institutes@iahp.org

Kushi Institute

Address:
198 Leland Road
Becket, MA 01223, USA
Contact Information:
Telephone: (800) 975-8744
International: (413) 623-6457
Email: programs@kushiinstitute.org

Acknowledgements

I wish to express my heartfelt appreciation to all those who have supported Bree and I over all these years.

First are my mother Lois Annett Gilker and my mother in law Muriel Schaff Scofield. The emotional support of these two woman was and is fundamental to our journey. My mother passed in 1988 and my mother in law will be turning 92 years young shortly. Two very amazing women and I am honoured to be related to them both.

Then there were the 26 woman from the ski village of St. Sauveur Des Monts, Quebec, Canada who volunteered to pattern Bree and help out with the stimulation program over a 2 ½ year period.

Thank you to my neighbor, when Bree was born, who turned out to be the mother-in-law of Hans Selye and brought me a copy of his book "Stress Without Distress" Little did I know at that time how much his work would mean in my life. She would babysit Bree. One of my first angels.

Mary Kett, my first Macrobiotic teacher, who took Bree and I under her wings and got me started with a solid foundation in macrobiotic cooking. She went with us to our first consultation with Michio Kushi and invited us into her residence in Boston many times. I first met Mary at The Institutes for the Achievement of Human Potential as she was a program director there before moving to Boston. Susanne Jensen, thank you for answering the phone at the Kushi Institute and connecting me with Mary .The synchronicity was powerful that day.

Micho and Aveline Kushi who introduced Macrobiotics to North America, pioneers in bringing organic foods and health food stores here. Because of the tireless work of both of these people, my daughter is still alive and healthy despite her devastating prognosis at birth. I will always remember covering Bree with a blanket while she was sleeping on a couch in one of the living rooms, and Michio's lectures are memorable.

The Macrobiotic community and the Kushi Institute. When I went to the Kushi Institute in 1997 to become qualified as a teacher of macrobiotics, I took Bree with me. This was a major undertaking. The Kushi Institute and the Macrobiotic community accepted us with open arms and worked with me to make this undertaking doable. Bree was with me in every lecture, cooking class, shiatsu class –all day and night and we did it.

Beverly Tuttle and Ed and Will Tuttle who provided a home for Bree and I during our first years in New Hampshire, thank you.

Zunk and Beth Buker. One day when I was out walking Bree in her stroller, Zunk drove up beside us, got out and asked –"Who is helping you". God Bless You Zunk. You did.

Marcel Vogel, who was my mentor the last 4 years of his life. Marcel Vogel had been a senior scientist at IBM for 27 years working with crystals. Every Wednesday morning after he had been to mass, he would work with us (crystal healing) over the phone. When he died, his wife gifted us with one of his healing crystals and I have been wearing a Vogel crystal for over 20 years now. I am blessed to have known him.

Lee Patterson who first edited this book and Sherbrooke Rogers who did later editing.

The Wright Family (Elize) who provided a home we could afford in New London for over 20 years. They kept the rent at a level I could afford and I looked after their house like it was my own. Thank you for that safe haven.

The Town Of New London, New Hampshire – so many people in the little town have supported Bree and I. They tend to keep an eye on us. We have been safe here for over 25 years. It is our home now. Thank you.

Margie Weathers – thank you, you saved us!!!

Janie Weber. Thank you for being at the other end of the phone through many years of challenges and always showing up for yard sales and moves. Those phone calls got me through many dark times. My spiritual sister.

Annie Miller, by coming with us, you made it possible for Bree and I to visit my birthplace on the Gaspe coast several times. I could not have managed these trips without you. You were such an amazing support and I have wonderful memories of you taking off with Bree (in her stroller) to the beach to find rocks. And Annie, you were there, thank God, when I crashed when Bree was 27 years.

Thank you Vicky and Tom Mills, Stephanie Wheeler, Dale Milne, Blair and Mathew McClay, Linda and Kenneth Miller, Margot Tatum, Stefan Timbrell, Harold Sofield. Vahan Sarkisian, Patricia Berkov , Sheridon Danforth

Susan Hankin-Berke-I am so very thankful to you. You fought long and hard for Bree rights and knowing you were there, took an incredible amount of stress off my shoulders.

Linda Howes, thank you for your friendship, guidance and the wonderful saunas.

And last, yet not least –Ben Harrold for being my computer expert and guide in getting all this information on the computer and published.

Except for my mother and mother-in- law, all these people were strangers when this journey with Bree began. These are the angels. Thank you all. In one way or another I could not of made the journey without you.

Bree is 10 years old (above), 17 years old (below)

Bree with her dogs, Sam and Mike

Bree is 6 years old with Sam (above left), Bree is in her 20's (above right)

Bree is in her 20's (middle left), Bree is 35 (middle right)

Bree is in her 20's (below)

192

Bree is in 20's (above and below)

Bree is 11 or 12

Bree is in her 30's

Bree is in her 30's

Bree is in her 30's

Printed in Poland
by Amazon Fulfillment
Poland Sp. z o.o., Wrocław